ISBN 978-1-331-97587-8
PIBN 10263138

1 MONTH OF FREE READING

at
www.ForgottenBooks.com

By purchasing this book you are eligible for one month membership to ForgottenBooks.com, giving you unlimited access to our entire collection of over 700,000 titles via our web site and mobile apps.

To claim your free month visit:
www.forgottenbooks.com/free263138

English
Français
Deutsche
Italiano
Español
Português

www.forgottenbooks.com

Mythology Photography **Fiction**
Fishing Christianity **Art** Cooking
Essays Buddhism Freemasonry
Medicine **Biology** Music **Ancient**
Egypt Evolution Carpentry Physics
Dance Geology **Mathematics** Fitness
Shakespeare **Folklore** Yoga Marketing
Confidence Immortality Biographies
Poetry **Psychology** Witchcraft
Electronics Chemistry History **Law**
Accounting **Philosophy** Anthropology
Alchemy Drama Quantum Mechanics
Atheism Sexual Health **Ancient History**
Entrepreneurship Languages Sport
Paleontology Needlework Islam
Metaphysics Investment Archaeology
Parenting Statistics Criminology
Motivational

THE OLD CHIMNEY STACKS

OF

EAST HADDAM,

MIDDLESEX COUNTY, CONNECTICUT,

BY

HOSFORD B. NILES,

Author of Genealogy of

THE NILES FAMILY.

———

NEW YORK:
LOWE & CO., Book and Job Printers
No. 210 Fulton Street.

———

1887

PREFACE.

This little book is largely a compilation and revision of serial chapters commenced by the author in the East Haddam *Advertiser*, in 1871, under the same title. It makes no pretensions to literary merit, and therefore has no claim upon the world at large. It is a brief record of the early history of East Haddam, and describes the prominent characters who figured therein, their toils, their perseverance, their homes—so many of which are represented by the old chimney piles dotted here and there all over the town. These numerous ruins of former homes suggested the work to the writer while taking the census of 1870. The information was gathered in fragments and this explains the fragmentary character of the work. It gives the genealogies of such old families as I have been able to obtain. That it may interest not only the present residents of the good old town, but the thousands who have wandered away and still claim it as their ancestral home, is the earnest wish of the

AUTHOR.

CONTENTS.

CHAPTER I.

CHAPTER XIX.

The Old Chimney Stacks of East Haddam.

CHAPTER I.

EARLY SETTLEMENT—CHAPMAN.

A stack of stones, a dingy wall,
  O'er which the shadows cling and creep,
A path on which no shadows fall,
  A door-step where long dock-leaves sleep;
A broken rafter in the grass,
  A sunken hearth-stone stained and cold;
Naught left but these, fair home, alas !
  And the dear memories of old.

Descriptions of the ruins of Tyre, and Nineveh, and Thebes, and those other ancient cities which flourished thousands of years ago, though often repeated, are always interesting. Notwithstanding they existed in a time so remote that the mind can scarcely fathom the dim distance, we love to contemplate their broken pillars and crumbling walls: to muse over their fallen towers and shattered hearth-stones; we love to unearth the buried secrets of their former existence, and reflect that all these relics were once associated with other men and women who had hopes, and impulses and aspirations like our own. The treasures which the dead leave behind them are always precious in our eyes, and their handiwork, their inventions, the evidences of their daily pursuits, are always full of interest. And it is with these facts in view that in a few chapters upon the old landmarks that form the only connecting links which bind us to our ancestors in whose footsteps we follow along the dim pathway of life, the writer hopes to interest those who cling to the memories of their native town.

East Haddam may be justly regarded as one of the oldest, as it is one of the largest towns in the State. Its diversified scenery, its bracing atmosphere, and its early historic associations have made the town an object of admiration to travellers, and of love to her sons and daughters. And she has reared many worthy sons who have graced the high pursuits of life; and of the virtue and beauty of her daughters she may well be proud.

The tract of land of which East Haddam is a part, extending from Chatham line to Chester Cove, and reaching six miles easterly and westerly from the river, was purchased from four Indian kings, in 1662, for thirty coats of a value not exceeding one hundred dollars. The tract thus purchased was taken up by twenty-eight persons, mostly young men from the vicinity of Hartford, who settled in the northern part of this land on the west side of the river.

About six years after, the privileges of a town were granted the colony, and the tract was called Haddam, from Haddam in England.

· This was about the twentieth town formed in the State. No settlement was made on the east side of the river till some two years later, or about 1670. All the inhabitants on both sides formed one society until 1700, when they formed two societies, but it was not till 1734 that the town was divided agreeably to the divisions of the societies; the west society retaining the name of Haddam while the east took the name of East Haddam. The first settlement of East Haddam was begun at Creek Row, about the year 1670, over two hundred years ago. The first house, it is said, stood a few rods northeast of the site where Mason Gates' house now stands. Quite a number of houses were erected in this vicinity, and were occupied by the Gateses, the Brainards, and the Cones, and the same family names are peculiar to this neighborhood. Fields, in his history, claims that the settlement at the Creek Row commenced in 1685, which appears to be an error, as from a document found in the colony records, it is certain that " Robert Chapman had a dwelling-house in East Haddam north of the Creek Row, in 1675 " It seems to be conceded on all sides that the settlement at Creek Row was first; then it must have commenced as early as 1670. Besides, as the land was purchased and the settlement commenced in Haddam in 1662, it is hardly supposable that twenty-three years would pass before any attempt was made to settle the east side of the river.

Among the earliest settlers of Saybrook was Robert Chapman. The name Chapman is of Saxon origin, meaning "chap-man," "market-man," a monger or merchant. A large class of surnames among the Anglo-Saxons is derived from trades or occupations. Robert Chapman came from Hull, in England, in 1635, and was one of the company sent over by Sir Richard Salsonstall to take possession of a large tract of land near the mouth of the Connecticut River, under the patent of Lord Say-and-Seal. He was then eighteen years old, and was one of the band of adventurers who established the fort at Saybrook. He was a man of exemplary piety. His parents were Puritans. That he was a person of influence in the town of Saybrook is evident from the fact that he was for many years Commissioner of Saybrook, and was elected as their deputy to the General Court, forty-three sessions. He was therefore a member of the Legislature of the State at more sessions than any other man from the settlement of Saybrook to the present time. Mr. Chapman was likewise a soldier, as we find by the records of the General Court at Hartford, Oct. 14, 1675:

Mr. Robert Chapman is by this Court appointed Capt'n of the Traine Band of Saybrook during the present commotion with the Indians.

· Mr. Chapman was a large land-holder, not only in Saybrook, Haddam, East Haddam, but in Hebron; there he owned forty-five hundred acres, which he received as one of the legatees of the Uncas This land was given by will, in equal parts, to his three sons, John, Robert and Nathaniel. He settled on a tract of land at Oyster River,

which has descended in the line of the youngest
son of each family, and is now occupied by George
W. Chapman, Esq., who is the youngest of the fifth
generation. Robert Chapman, Jr., second son of
the first settler, was born in Saybrook in 1646.
He owned at his death over two thousand acres of
land in Saybrook, East Haddam and Hebron.
Robert Chapman, 3d, was born April 19, 1675, and
was one of the first settlers in East Haddam. He
was a large land-holder. One of his daughters
married a soldier of Haddam Neck, and received
two hundred acres of land as her portion, which
has remained in the family to the present time, the
owners now being two brothers, W. C. and H. N.
Selden. Their farm is inclosed by over five miles
of street fence—one hundred acres being sur-
rounded by highways. James Wilbur Chapman,
grandson of the last named Robert Chapman, and
of the seventh generation from the first settlers,
was born August 8, 1802, and resided on, and
was the owner of the farm which has remained in
the family ever since it was first taken up. It has
been deeded but once, and then to Robert W.,
having heretofore descended to the heirs by will.

Caleb Chapman was also a large land-holder in
East Haddam. He gave his land to his three sons,
Timothy, Ozias and Timothy 2d. The latter settled on the spot where Amasa Day now lives. The
farm was subsequently sold to Phineas Gates, who
was related to the Chapman family by marriage.
He sold it to Julius Chapman, after whose death it
was sold at auction and purchased by Mr. Day.

Timothy settled where Robert Day now lives; Ozias where Wm. S. Gates lives. Ozias had nine sons and six daughters. Joseph Emmons, and Mr. and Mrs. Daniel Lord are among his direct descendants. Sylvester, the oldest of Ozias' sons, acquired considerable property from his wife. He lived in the first house north of the Congregational Church, which was then considered quite a stately residence. He kept a store, which stood a few rods south of his house. He was also a Justice of the Peace in the town for a number of years. John Chapman, the eldest son of Robert, the first settler, settled at Goodspeed's Landing, his home standing on the spot where the Gelston House now stands. He established the ferry across the river at that place, which has always remained private property, and until within a few years retained its original name of Chapman's Ferry.

CHAPTER II.

EAST HADDAM LANDING.

The first dwelling house in East Haddam Land
ing was erected in 1743. A market for produce
was opened about the same time, and a storehouse
built, which stood on the spot now occupied by
Dr. Harris' barn in front of Tyler's store. A large
storehouse stood on the site of the store and just
back of the ledge of rocks stood a hotel with a
piazza on the river front. During the revolutionary war many soldiers on their way from the east
ern part of the State to the North River forces
made this a favorite route and stopped at this pub
lic house. Later, the house in which Ashbel Ray
now lives was the principal public house, and called
"The Blacksmith's Arms." The name was painted
in rude letters upon a swing sign, suspended high
between two posts that may have formed the original gallows of Haman. It was further illustrated
by a bent muscular arm, wielding a blacksmith's
hammer. The present generation remember the
Landing as a beautiful village with a row of fine
houses, at the summit of a gently rising green, and
two neat white fences making two parallel roads
and terraces, which, in contrast with the bold,
abrupt mountain behind presented one of the most
attractive and picturesque scenes on one of the
most charming of rivers.

The most central, perhaps, of the dwellings, was the one alluded to above. It was then the residence of Capt. James Green, and its high stone stoop facing both ways bespoke hospitality almost as plainly as its gaily painted sign. The brick house next north of this is a fine building of more recent date, and belonged to the Captain's son, Timothy. Next beyond stands the former residence of his daughter Nancy (Mrs. Jared Spencer, Esq.,) and further on (the site of the bank building) was the forge and then the residence of Oliver Green. The next house to the "Arms" on the south side was the residence of Capt. Green's brother.in-law, Mr. Thomas Marshall. Next south lived his son Richard ; next to that his daughter Hannah, Mrs. Joseph Hungerford. These buildings have been metamorphosed into the Maple Wood Music Seminary, and of the two generations who made music and uproar (opera) there, is now but an occasional visitor. Here then in the midst of his children lived Captain James Green, and just over the way, as first postmaster of East Haddam, he presided over that *event* in New England—the mail arrival and distribution. His descendants have nearly all left their native town, and have prospered and maintained the honor of the family name in the busy world of trade and progress, but they have never forgotten the old town, to which they return every summer, like pilgrims to their native shrine. The family genealogy will be given in another chapter.

Down near the steamboat dock Noah Buckley

erected a large store and built up quite an extensive wholesale and importing trade with the West Indies. He owned a large farm in Millington, where he raised mules, which he used to send out in his vessels and exchange for molasses, sugar, etc. He bought the brick hotel built by Samuel Lord, where the Champion House stands, and accumulated considerable money. Like many others, he was wooed and won by the tempter in the person of Roswell C. Peck, who induced him to invest in a banking speculation in New York.

He lost his property and went to Chicago, then in its infancy, and again became rich and well known as the " Miser Money Lender."

Ship building was begun at the Landing some time during the Revolutionary War, and formed quite an important branch of business till within a few years. Several coasting and generally two or three sea vessels were owned here. In the year 1815, there were launched from this yard two brigs and three schooners. A few years later this branch of business was carried on, but less extensively, at Chapman's Ferry. At this time there was a general store near the Center Congregational Church, on the main road from Moodus to Hadlyme. Shad fishing has been carried on to quite an extent since the early settlement of the town, and for the last seventy years has been quite profitable. Previous to this time this delicacy was hardly appreciated.

Salmon River, which enters the Connecticut at the Landing, derives its name from the large num ber of salmon formerly caught from it, but for

many years none have been found, and the celebrated fishermen at the Cove have now to rely on
the small fry.

The original settlers of East Haddam laid out
the town into nine sections of three-fourths a mile
square, and the roads running north and south
were made that distance apart as boundaries for
the same. In this " lay out," convenience and
topography seem to have been of little account.
Any one familiar with our roads will readily notice
this observance of distance. The same distance is
also observed to a certain extent in the roads running east and west.

"East Haddam and Colchester Turnpike," extending from " East Haddam Landing to Colchester
meeting house," was granted in October, 1809, with
a capital stock of $6,288. About the year 1806
a post-road was established from Middletown,
through Chatham, to East Haddam Landing, and
thence to New London. A turnpike from Nor
wich to New Haven, through East Haddam, was
granted in 1817.

CHAPTER III.

MILLINGTON.

According to Field's History, the first settler in Millington was Jonathan Beebe, from New London, who settled by the Long Pond about 1704, and was soon joined by several persons, who have now descendants in East Haddam. They settled west of the pond, on the hill about the Hayward farm, recently owned by Rowland Allen. Some traces of their houses still remain, yet most of them are completely obliterated. Except at this spot, there were no inhabitants in Millington until about 1732–3–4, when families moved into it by the name of Arnold, Barnes, Brainard, Chapman, Church, Cone, Emmons, Fuller, Gates, Olmsted and Spencer, from East Haddam parish; of Harvey and Hungerford, from Hadlyme; of Clarke, from Haddam; of Greaves, from Colchester; and Stewart, from Voluntown; Daniel Smith, from some part of Plymouth Colony; Lemuel Griffin, from Lyme, and Thomas Fox, from Colchester, settled here not long after. Millington Society was for a number of years the most thickly settled and influential portion of the town. In 1810 there were 172 dwelling houses in that Society, while in the first Society there were but 167. There were also a number of stores and a large local business carried on, Millington being the centre of trade for quite a large tract of country.

With scarcely a solitary exception, those who now remain are tillers of the rugged soil, and are noted for their frugality, industry and hospitality. But alas ! the growing tendency of the age to centralize in the cities and villages, and the tempting allurements of the South and West have shorn the town of much of her ancient renown. Many of her children sleep in her hillside graves, and many more' have wandered far and wide ; but none of them find happier hours than when they return to meet the hearty welcome of their native home. Sixty years ago the Middle or Green School District numbered 69. The same district now has about one-third of that number. At the same time, the West District numbered 51 ; it now numbers but 13.

The Old Chimney Stacks form quite a prominent feature of the landscape. In Millington, the tan-yard at McLean's, which once carried on a large business, is now a mass of ruins. Just east of the yard is the cellar over which stood the house of Nathan Beebe, an uncle of Manly, and great uncle of Sherman Beebe.

Sherman broke loose from the old farm and went to California in its early days, where he prospered, and returned to buy the large farm he now occupies in North Millington. He has seven sons, and is one of the towns heaviest tax-payers.

Just west of the tan-yard, near the Dutton barn (so-called), stood another house, and a short distance north, on the. Colchester road, are ruins which mark the residences of families of Elys and Fullers.

A half-mile south, on the corner, stands what is called the old Auger Stack, and farther on, near Alexander's shop, lived Deacon Diodate Lord.

The Austin Beebe house is comparatively a late ruin. This corner, now so deserted, seems to have been quite a settlement many years ago. A store was kept here by Timothy Spencer, and just north, on the old stony road leading to Long Pond, lived Isham Fuller and Dr. Nye. The latter moved away and afterwards gained considerable renown. The old house below Deacon Ackley's was built by one Williams, one of the early settlers. "Wall street," the old road running north from the Green, is now entirely deserted. The store built by Ephraim Warner, near the entrance, and where considerable business was carried on, was long since converted into Mr. Joseph Arnold's horse-shed. A short distance north was Ephraim Warner's house, and further north, but short distances apart, stood the Marsh house, the Burke house, the Ephraim Arnold house, the Plum house, the Hall house, the Beri Gates house, and the Wickham house.

Here large families were raised, and the street formed an important thoroughfare of the town. Now, grass and weeds grow over its travelled paths ; green mounds of house-leek, and rude piles of stone and mortar are the only evidences of former civilization. A goodly portion of the north part of Millington Society was owned and occupied by the Arnolds—Ephraim, John and Joseph. The latter was the father of Isaiah Arnold, and the grandfather of Samuel and Joseph, Jr. Samuel has four children living, viz.: Fluvia, married L. W. Cone ; Nancy, married Charles Miner ; Eme line, married W. L. Fuller; William lives in Brooklyn, Long Island.

Joseph, Jr., has one son, Joseph H., who married Harriet M. Swan, who died early in 1879. She left two children, Dwight and Fred, but the latter has since died.

The old road leading southeast from Millington Green, or rather the road branching off from this to Chapman's Mills, was in early days a main thoroughfare, upon which several families lived, but which is now lonely, deserted and almost impassible—its silence seldom broken save by an occasional ox-cart rattling over the stones, or by the sharp crack of the hunter's gun. The terminus of the road, however, presents attractions which richly repay a rough and toilsome journey. The wild and romantic beauty of the scenery about Chapman's Mills is not surpassed by those historic spots about which volumes have been written. The pond here is the source of Eight-Mile River, which empties into Hamburg Cove. It starts with two separate outlets from a rocky island, and joins about a half-mile below. Both streams leap down rocky ledges over one hundred feet high, with a roar that can be heard far away. The grist mill, upon the right branch, has gone to ruin, but the saw mill has been kept in running order. Between the two mills, on the island, stands the house now occupied by Cyrus W. Chapman, so that the place still retains the name of its original owner. It was owned and occupied for several years by Col. A. T. Niles, and here the writer spent many " happy hours of childhood."

Following the river from the point of its quiet and peaceful reunion, at the foot of the Falls, down over Kettle Hill, so called from the unfathomable circular holes in its rocky crest; along the old coal-pit, whose once black pit is now white with birches; by the rough chimney pile which marks the little house where Benjamin Banning raised nineteen children, whose exploits at "diving from mullin stalks into the dew" surprised many a morning teamster ; through the Hop-Yard, with its tall evergreens, its frowning precipices, and its Devil's Cave, and we reach the " Plain " with a feeling that we have journeyed through the wilderness and finally reached the promised land. The " Plain " forms the southeast corner of the town, and a part of Millington Society.

The traveller here finds a pleasing landscape, with thrifty and well-cultivated farms, which were originally owned by settlers from the adjoining town of Lyme. The old chimney stack, which occupies so prominent a position just north of Nathan Jewett's, was known as the Griffin house, where lived Edward Dorr Griffin, D. D., President of Williamstown College. The old Jewett homestead is just beyond the bridges over the Lyme

Line.   Returning to Millington Green, and taking
the Hadlyme road south, we soon come to the old
Spencer chimney stack, where lived Gen. Joseph.
Spencer, of Revolutionary fame, who will receive
notice in a future letter.   Here, too, David Brain
ard, the celebrated missionary, spent several years
of his youth.   Nearly opposite the Spencer place
is the Williams' place, where lived Dr. Datus Williams, a prominent physician of the town.   He
afterwards moved in near the Center Church,
where he died a few years since.   His son, George
G., President of the Chemical Bank, New York
City, has enlarged and beautified the place till it is
now one of the finest in the town.   He occupies it
as a summer residence.   A few rods south of the
Spencer place is the Lyman place, where Dr.
Lyman lived, who was for many years pastor of
the Millington Church.   In the woods, near Bald
Hill, about two miles south of Millington Green,
are the remains of an old house where lived one
Will Fox.   Near by is the Oakley house, where
lived Dr. Root, father of Francis G. Root, of Leesville.   Dr. Root afterwards lived at the Warner
house, on Potash Hill.

CHAPTER IV

Moodus.

Moodus is a contraction of the Indian word Machimoodus, meaning " place of noises." Formerly the place was also called Mechanicsville, and was quite insignificant as compared with Millington and the Landing, till within a few years. Now it is the most industrious and thickly settled portion of the town. An old teacher gives a description of the place in 1815 :

Assuming the boundaries to be the house of Wilbur Chapman on the west, Wigwam Brook on the south, the Alanson Gates house on the east, and the Methodist Church on the north. There were eleven dwellings and other buildings as follows :

The house of Mr. Chapman was then occupied by his grandfather, Robert B. Its roof was flat and covered with earth, from which sprang up a sparse vegetation and protected by a balustrade. There was a square-roofed building on the opposite side, then occupied by Erastus Chapman. These were white, standing out in strong contrast of color from all other buildings in the vicinity. On the stream just south of the road, and approached by a gate near where the road to the Neptune Twine Mills is now opened, was a saw-mill, and just below a carding mill and clothiers works, in one of which the rolls were prepared for the wheel, and in the other, the cloth was colored and dressed.

East of the Chapman house, on the same side, was the house of Ozias Chapman. Next came the house near the stream, occupied by ' Old Mr. Hurd,' who was on active duty at the Grist Mill when over ninety years of age. The stream

was crossed by a bridge of planks a little above the present
arch.   Its position necessitated a curve in the road as we
approached it, and an unfortunate young man who had passed
an evening with a young lady in the neighborhood, on taking a
straight course for home, instead of following the curve, found
himself with a broken arm among the rocks in the stream.

East of the bridge, occupying the ground where Smith's
(Bodies') factory now stands, was the grist mill, with its overshot
wheel, where boys waiting for their grists would look upon the
mimic rainbows, and fancy their resemblance to those described
in their ' American Preceptor,' as rising from the spray of
Niagara.

" Passing east to ' The Plain ' the next building was a dilap-
dated old house occupied by Phineas Gates, which soon gave
way to the dwelling occupied by Mr. Day.   Across the street,
in the house now occupied by Mr. Richmond, was Dr. Joseph
Cone.   This was only about two-thirds of its present dimen-
sions.   Quite a distance south was a small brown house, and a
little south of that a small old house and a shoemaker's shop,
and small building on the hillside sloping towards Wigwam
Brook.   East, on the Bashan Road, was the Alanson Gates
(Daniel Lord) house, unpainted and the grounds unadorned.
The street through the ' Plain ' was wider than it is now by
nearly the depths of the yards on the east side, and was wholly
destitute of trees.   From Mr. Day's the road ' up town '
descended the hill in a northerly direction.   The stream was
crossed by a bridge similar to the one described, and the road
wound around and came out at the foot of the hill south of the
cemetery.   Just north of the bridge referred to was a path
running to the east parallel with the stream, which passed a
long, low building known as the ' Old Malt House,' then
curved and terminated at the grist mill, which stood where the
twine mill now stands.   This path was the only approach to
the mill, and was so obstructed by a point of rocks that it
could be passed only on horseback, and then the boy had to
keep to the middle of it or his grist would be pushed off by the
rocks, or the corner of the mill.   On the knoll, north of the

mill, stood a one-story, gabled roof house, for the accommoda-
tion of the miller. This finishes the catalogue of buildings in
Moodus in 1815.

The first step in advance was the erection of the
stone mill and store, and other necessary buildings.

The first school house in Moodus was built in
1828. Previous to that the children were divided
between Red Lane and " Up Town " districts.

Moodus, at the present time, is the center and
most populous portion of the town. This has
arisen from its fine water privileges, on which have
been built several large cotton factories.

CHAPTER V.

Moodus Noises.

The Indians which inhabited the place were numerous, of a fierce and warlike character, and were remarkable for the worship of evil spirits. They called the town Machimoodus, which means, in English "the place of noises." A very suitable name, because of the noises or quakings which were familiarly called "Moodus Noises." The noises sometimes resemble the slow thunder, at others the rattling of musketry or the discharge of cannon. They have been the subject of much dis cussion, and many theories have been advanced about their origin. An old Indian's reason was that "the Indian's God was very angry because the Englishman's God came here. Many persons credit the report of a transient person named Doctor Steele, from Great Britain, who, hearing about these noises, came here and dug up two pearls, which he called carbuncles. He told the people the noises would be discontinued for many years, as he had taken away their cause, but as he had discovered other smaller ones, they would be heard again in the process of time. Notwithstanding the absurdity of this prophecy, it seemed to prove itself correct, for the noises did cease for many years, but finally returned. The Doctor was a mysterions sort of a person, and in order to allay the

fears of the simple and terrified inhabitants, arising
by reason of the noises, attempted many magical
operations, and for this purpose took possession of
a blacksmith's shop, which stood on the hill northwest of the Atlantic Duck Mill, in which he worked
night and day, excluding all light so as to prevent
any prying curiosity from interfering with his
occult operations. He claimed that the carbuncle
had grown to a great size in the bowels of the
rocks and must be removed. The Doctor finally
departed, and has never been heard of since.
From this circumstance arose this ballad, by John
G. C. Brainard, editor of the Hartford *Mirror*

MACHIT–MOODUS.

See you, upon the lonely moor,
    A crazy building rise?
No hand dares venture to open the door—
No footstep treads its dangerous floor
    No eve in its secret pries.

Now why is each crevice stopped so tight?
    Say, why the bolted door?
Why glimmers at midnight the forge's light?
All day is the anvil at rest, but at night
    The flames of the furnace roar.

Is it to arm the horses' heel,
    That the midnight anvil rings?
Is it to mould the ploughshare's steel,
Or is it to guard the wagon's wheel,
    That the smith's sledge hammer swings?

The iron is bent, and the crucible stands
    With alchymy boiling up ;
Its contents are mixed by unknown hands,
And no mortal fire e'er kindled the brands
    That heated that cornered cup.

O'er Moodus river a light has glanced,
    On Moodus hills it shone ·
On the granite rocks the rays have danced,
And upwards those creeping lights advanced
    Till they met on the highest stone.

Oh ! that is the very wizard place,
    And now is the wizard hour,
By the light that was conjured up to trace,
E'er the star that falls can run its race,
    The seat of the earthquake's power.

By that unearthly light, I see
    A figure strange, alone,
With magic circlet on his knee,
And, decked with Satan's symbols, he
    Seeks for the hidden stone.

Now upward goes that gray old man,
    With mattock, bar and spade—
The summit is gained and the toil begun,
And deep by the rock where the wild lights run,
    The magic trench is made.

Loud, and yet louder was the groan,
    That sounded wide and far ;
And deep and hollow was the moan
That rolled around the bedded stone
    Where the workman plied his bar.

Then upward streamed the brilliant light—
    It streamed o'er crag and stone ;
Dim looked the stars and the moon that night,
But when morning came in her glory bright,
    The man and the jewel were gone.

But woe to the bark in which he flew
    From Moodus rocky shore—
Woe to the captain and woe to the crew,
That ever the breath of life they drew
    When that dreadful freight they bore.

Where is that crew and vessel now ?
    Tell me their state who can,
The wild waves dashed o'er the sinking bow
Down, down to the fathomless depths they go—
    To sleep with a sinful man.

The carbuncle lies in the deep sea,
    Beneath the mighty wave ;
But the light shines up so gloriously
That the sailor looks pale and forgets his glee,
    When he crosses the wizard's grave.

Many theories have been advanced as to the cause of these noises. One is that there is a subterranean passage leading from a large cave near Mt. Tom to the sea, and that the noises are produced by certain delicate combinations of wind and tide. A more reasonable explanation of their cause is, that there exist mineral or chemical combinations, which explode many feet below the earth's surface. The jar produced by the noises is like that of exploded gunpowder.

CHAPTER VI.

MIDDLESEX COUNTY.

Middlesex County was formed in the year 1785. Previous to that time the inhabitants of the several towns repaired to the courts in the counties to which they previously belonged, when a resort to law was necessary to obtain redress. Several gentlemen from these towns appear, from the records of the Colony and State of Connecticut, to have seats in the Courts of Hartford, New London, and New Haven counties, previous to the formation of Middlesex County. Hon. Joseph Spencer, of East Haddam, was Justice of the Quorum for Hartford County from May 1778 to 1779. As previously mentioned, Gen. Dyer Throop, of East Haddam, was the first Judge of the Middlesex County Court.

Among the Justices of the Quorum from the same county there were from East Haddam, Jabez Chapman, Esq., from 1795 to 1802 ; Col. Eliphelet Holmes, from 1802 to 1817; Col. Josiah Griffin, from 1817 to 1818.

The State's Attornies for the county from its formation to the year 1820 were : Hon. Asher Miller, of Midletown, from 1785 to 1794; Hon. Samuel W. Dana, of Middletown, from 1794 to 1797 ; Hon. J. O. Moseley, of East Haddam, from 1797 to 1805 ; Hon. S. T. Hosmer, of Middletown, from 1805 to

1815; Matthew T. Russel, Esq., of Middletown, from 1815 to 1818; Major Andre Andrews, of Middletown, from 1818.

The Sheriffs of the county were: William W Parsons, of Middletown, from 1785 to 1791; Enoch Parsons, Esq., of Middletown, from 1791 to 1818; J. Lawrence Lewis, Esq., of Middletown; from 1818 to 1827; Gideon Higgins, Esq., of East Haddam from 1827 to 1830; Linus Coe, of Middletown from 1830 to 1839; Charles Arnold, of Haddam, from 1839 to 1845; Charles Stevens, of Clinton from 1845 to 1851. Since that time the office has been held by Dr. Burr, of Killingworth, Curtis Bacon, of Middletown, Charles Snow, of Deep River, J. I. Hutchinson, of Essex, the present incumbent, and Arba Hyde.

The Probate District of East Haddam was formed in October, 1741, and embraced the towns of Haddam, East Haddam, Colchester, Hebron, and that part of Middletown (now Chatham) lying south of the Salmon River. Haddam was taken from this and united to a new district in 1752, and Hebron in 1789. Colchester has remained a part of this district till within a few years. The first Judge of this Court was Hon. John Bulkley, of Colchester, from 1741 to 1753; Hon. James Spencer, of East Haddam, from 1753 to 1789. In 1776, while the latter was out of the State, Daniel Brainard, Esq., of East Haddam, was appointed to act as Judge, while Judge Spencer was connected with the armies of the United States. Isaac Spencer,

Esq., of East Haddam, succeeded James Spencer, and held the office for twenty-nine years.

The following persons were appointed Justices of the Peace, or, as they were formerly called, Commissioners, for East Haddam, at the time of the formation of the County: Gen, Dyer, Throop, Col. Jabez Chapman, Israel Spencer, Timothy Gates.

In 1815 there were 421 families in town, divided among the religious denominations as follows : Congregationalists, 286; Episcopalians, fifty-five; Baptists, seventy-two; Methodists, eight.

Our great-grandfathers drew rather nicer distinctions between right and wrong than their innocent descendants of the present day. A little of the old leaven than with which they vitalized their laws would not be unhealthy for present use, while many of their enactments would be somewhat impracticable. I copy from an old *Counecticut Register*, dated 1793, an " Act to be read at the opening of every Freemen's Meeting."

" *Be it enacted, etc.*, That if any person shall endeavor to persuade or influence any other person or persons in giving their vote or suffrage for any Member of the Legislature by offering to any person or persons any written vote or votes for that purpose without being first thereto requested, such person so offending shall pay a fine of forty shillings, for the use of the Town Treasury."

Following the above are several " Acts " of like import.

Here are some of the Acts for putting in execution good and wholesome laws for restraining irreligious practices and disorders ·

"*Be it enacted, etc.*, That the Selectmen from time to time shall diligently enquire of all Householders how they are furnished with Bibles, and if, upon such enquiry, any Householder be found without one Bible at least, then the Selectmen shall warn the said Householder forthwith to procure one Bible at least for the use and benefit of their Families respectively; and if the same be neglected, then the said selectman shall make return thereof to the next authority, who may deal with such Householder's Family according to the directions of the Law relating to the educating and governing of children. * * And the Constables and Grand Jurymen in the respective Towns shall, on the evenings after the Lord's Day and other public Days of Religious Solemnity, walk the street and duly search all places suspected for harboring or entertaining any People or Persons assembled contrary to law."

Another act provides that "it shall be the duty of the Selectmen to see that all families are supplied with a suitable number of Orthodox Catechisms and other good Books of practical Godliness and the like."

The circumstances under which the early settlers were placed rendered it necessary that they should be trained in the use of firearms, and local military organizations were to be found in all parts of the country. In the earlier history of the town companies of East Haddam belonged to the 12th Regiment. In 1776 East Haddam and Colchester were formed into the 24th Regiment. A company from Hadlyme belonged to the 33d Regiment.

The different commanders of the 24th Regiment from East Haddam were Gen. Dyer Throop, Jabez Chapman, David B. Spencer, Gen. Epaph Champion, Jon. O. Moseley, Josiah Griffin and Jonah Gates.

In 1816 there was a general reorganization of the Militia throughout the State, which was preserved till within a few years. It is within the memory of our young men that " Training Days," were great events in the history of the town, from which all other events were dated. Soldiers with their tall hats and taller plumes, dressed in showy uniforms, met in companies in the different societies in town, once a year, where they were drilled in the manual of arms—marched in sections, platoons, and by company, and dismissed after several general discharges of musketry. How the boys reverenced those famous soldiers! The greatest scalawag in town, upon these occasions, was transformed into a hero, in their eyes, as long as he wore the regimentals. Among the early captains of the companies were ·

EAST HADDAM NORTH COMPANY.—Samuel Olmsted, Stephen Cone, Thomas Gates, Daniel Gates, Caleb Chapman, John Percival, Joshua Percival, Gen. Dyer Throop, Jonathan Olmsted, Jonathan

Kilbourn, Jehial Fuller, Levi Palmer, Abner Hale Dea. Caleb Gates, Elisha Cone, Darius Gates, Darius Brainard, William Palmer.

EAST HADDAM SOUTH COMPANY.—John Chapman, John Holmes, Nathan Smith, Jabez Chapman, Daniel Cone, Bezaliel Brainard, Dea. James Gates, Matthew Smith, Maj. Daniel Cone, Col. David Spencer, Elijah Ackley, Gen. E. Champion, Jeremiah Smith, Robert Cone, Samuel P. Lord, Richard Green, Joseph Church, Samuel Crowel.

MILLINGTON NORTH COMPANY.—Joseph Arnold William Church, John Willey, Enoch Brainard, Amasa Dutton, John Arnold, Noadiah Emmons, Nathaniel Lord, Maj. N. Emmons, Aaron Fox, Oliver Church, Diodate Lord, Hezekiah Loomis, Manley Beebe.

MILLINGTON SOUTH COMPANY.—Jared Spencer John McCall, Aaron Cleaveland, Jonah Cone, William Cone, Ebenezer Dutton, Nathan Jewett, John Chapman, Joseph Gates, Robert Anderson, Amos Randal, Col. Josiah Griffin, Diodate Jones, Samuel Morgan, Gardner Gallop, Uriah Spencer, David G. Otis, Jon. Beckwith, Berah Beckwith.

HADLYME COMPANY.—Dea. Chris. Holmes, Eph. Fuller, Eb. Spencer, John Shaw, Col. Eliph Holmes, Zach. Hungerford, Abraham Willey, Eb. Holmes, Jab. Comstock, Chas. Spencer, Newton Marsh, Ben. Crosby, Rob. Hungerford, Chauncey Beckwith, Calvin Comstock, Ozias Holmes.

(The above is taken largely from Field's History.)

CHAPTER VII.

The First Congregational Society.

The inhabitants on this side of the river began to act as an ecclesiastical society about 1700. The first church formed January 6th, 1704. First meeting house stood near Isaac Ackley's in the street. It was thirty-two feet square, and was five years in building; used twenty-three years. Second house, finished in 1728. It stood in the street, near Henry Thompson's. The third, or present church, was dedicated November 27th, 1794, and to this day wears the same coat of shingles. The first minister in the Society was Rev. Stephen Hosmer, who died June 18th, 1749, aged 70. He lived nearly opposite Vine B. Star's, at the Creek Row.

The following was copied from a manuscript in the possession of Joshua Green, M. D., of Groton Massachusetts ·

A DISTICH,

Occasioned by ye marriage of Mr. Robert Hosmer, of East Haddam, and Mary Green, the only daughter of Timothy Green, of New London (Oct. ve 31st, 1745.)

COMPOSED BY HER FATHER.

Thro' the Divine faVour, both the Brides-grooms' parents and ye Bride's Parents are yet living, and consented to this marriage.

I.

You now in marriage have joined hands
  And are become Bridegroom and Bride,
'Tis God who has inclined your hearts
  So very near to be ally'd.

II.

Having passed through your SingleState
  And entered on ye married one,
New Duties you'll find springing up
  And always calling to be done.

II.

And now, my Son, I you Intreat
  Be ever tender to your wife.
And you, my daughter, I exhort,
  To love your husband as y'r Life.

IV.

May both of you Examples be,
  And be adorned with every Grace ;
Be circumspect in y'r whole Walk
  And know ye duties of y'r Place.

I wish you Joy in this y'r Choice,
  And Sorrow too, if God sees best,
Which shall promote y'r real Good,
  And fitt you for eternal rest.

And Isaac took Rebecca, and she became his wife, and he loved her.—*Gen.* xxiv., 67.

There was a marriage in Cana of Galilee, and both Jesus was called and his disciples to the marriage.—*John* ii., 1-2.

And her neighbors and her cousins rejoiced with her.— *Luke* i, 5-8.

Rev. Joseph Fowler succeeded Mr. Hosmer. He was born in Lebanon; installed May 15th, 1751; died 1771, aged 48.

Rev. Elijah Parsons, born at Northampton, Mass. Graduated Yale 1768; installed October 28th, 1772; died January 17th, 1827, aged 79.

His son Isaac Parsons, succeeded him. Born in Southampton, Mass. Graduated Yale 1811; ordained October 23d, 1816; dismissed April 1st, 1856; died August 21st, 1868, at the house of Robt. W. Chapman, in Moodus.

He was succeded by Rev. Silas W. Robbins. He was born in Dorset, Vt.; graduated at Wesleyan University, in 1847; installed October 16th, 1856; dismissed 1871, He is now located at Rockville, Connecticut.

The present pastor is Rev. Solomon McCall who is a native of Lebanon, Ct.; graduated at Yale 1851; was pastor in Old Saybrook, Ct., from December, 1853 to November, 1871; installed in East Haddam June 5th, 1872.

CHAPTER VIII.

MILLINGTON ECCLESIASTICAL SOCIETY.

The following is the first record of the society of Millington : "At a society meeting warned according to directions of ye law, to be holden on ye third day of December, Anno Domini, 1733, at ye mansion house of Jonathan Chapman, in ye parish of Millington, in ye town of Haddam, John Bulkley was chosen Moderator at said meeting, and James Cone was chosen Clerk and sworn to a faithful discharge of his office by John Bulkley, justice of the peace. Samuel Emmons, Samuel Olmstead, and Matthias Fuller were chosen society committee. Also, it was voted that ye society will engage some suitable person to preach ye gospel to ye people in this society ; also, it was voted that the committee as above said shall apply themselves to ye Rev. Mr. Hosmer for his advice and directions in their endeavors to engage some person to preach among them as aforesaid."

The meetings of the society were held at the house of Mr. John Chapman for a number of years. As near as I can ascertain, his house stood near the lower part of the hop yard. The Rev. Mr. Hosmer, alluded to in the above report, was at that time pastor of the church in the first society. It appears by the records that the society made several applications for preachers before they succeeded in having a permanent settlement. The first religious services were held for a considerable period in a house standing near the "Burke House," on Wall street. It appears that the first call for preaching was given a Mr. Williams, for at a meeting held December, 1734, it is recorded, "that ye society will not give Mr. Williams forty shillings a day for preaching ye gospel to ye people in said society" At a society meeting held March 7th, 1735, it was voted that the committee be instructed to engage the services of the Rev. Mr. Hosmer, and, in case he refused, to apply to the Rev. Nathaniel Brainard.

At the same time there was voted the sum of seventy pounds a year for the support of the ministry. June 30th, 1736, the society applied to the Rev. Mr. Brown, and engaged him to preach the gospel for two months at thirty-five shillings a day. At a subsequent meeting, held in September, 1736, the society voted a call to Rev. Timothy Symmes, and as an inducement it was "further voted that ye society will give Mr. Symmes three hundred and twenty pounds towards his settlement, and thirty pounds in labor towards building him a house, also one hundred pounds salary and find him his firewood ; and that ye society will clear, break up, fence, and sow with wheat, two acres of land, the first year Mr. Symmes is an ordained minister in said society, and also plant out one hundred of apple trees on said land ye next spring after it is sowed with wheat."

This call was accepted by Mr. Symmes in a letter dated October 26th, 1736. It appears from the records of these early days of the society that the good people were early risers and transacted their business in the early part of the day, for their society meetings were generally adjourned " to ye hour of eight of ye clock in the morning."

It seems that perfect harmony among the members of the society was as rare a virtue a hundred years ago as now. For a number of years the society suffered by a division arising from a difference, partially doctrinal, but more from different views in regard to forms. Finally, at a society meeting, held the 17th of April, 1776, "it was voted not to oppose a number of said parish who call themselves Old Fathers and Dissenters of New England, if they should apply to the Hon. General Assembly of this colony to be made a district Ecclesiastical Society."

Several legacies were granted to the society from time to time. The first one was bequeathed by Mr. Samuel Gates, who died August 21st, 1801, of two hundred and sixty dollars.

A farm was also given by Mr. Simeon Chapman, who died March 31st, 1813 ; but to be used by his children during life. This bequest amounted to four thousand two hundred and eighty dollars.

A legacy of fourteen hundred and forty dollars was also left by Thomas Beebe, who died June 6th, 1816. He was a son of Dr. Beebe, who lived a short distance southeast of the Estabrook house.

A part of the old chimney still remains. Dr. Beebe was a strong Tory during the Revolutionary War, and made himself so obnoxious that a party headed by Capt. Aaron Fox took him from the house one night and gave him a coat of tar and feathers.

Thomas, the legator, was not religiously inclined, and it is said that he did not make his bequest because he loved the society more, but that he loved his family less. Capt. Aaron Fox was for a number of years captain of the Millington militia. His grandfather, Ebenezer, was one of the earliest settlers of Millington. He was one of three brothers who came from England. One of them settled in Massachusetts, one in Rhode Island, and Ebenezer in Foxtown, where he built a log house near the old house built by Aaron Fox, and now owned by Matthew Fox. The brothers occasionally visited each other, taking the journey through the wilderness on horseback, their wives riding behind them.

A portion of the house where Ebeneezer, a son of Aaron, recently died, was built by Enoch Arnold, about one hundred and fifty years ago. People came from a great distance to the raising. It was covered with white-oak clap boards, securely fastened with wrought nails. Two of the original rooms still remain. The Old Chimney Stack, just west of Charles Swan's, is what remains of a house built and occupied by Brockway Beebe, and later by Josiah W. Willey. Turner Miner came from New London about the year 1770, and erected a house where Charles Swan lives. The place was subsequently bought by Rufus Swan, who gave it to his son Wheeler. Turner Miner married a daughter of General Joseph Spencer by his second wife. The wife of Deacon Jeremiah Hutchins and Mrs. James Stranahan are daughters of Mr. Miner, and consequently granddaughters of Gen. Spencer. Rev. Nathaniel Miner, who preached in Millington for a number of years, is a nephew of Turner Miner.

The old Estabrook house, on Millington Green, and long known as the parsonage, was built by Rev. Hobert Estabrook, who came from Canterbury and settled in Millington. Preached and died there in 1766. Hobert 2, born 1748, at Millington. Moved to Lebanon, N. H., and died in 1839, aged 91. He married Hannah Paddleford, who died May 24th, at Chatham, Conn.

Children :

Hannah, married Hurlbert Swan ; she died September 18th, 1831, aged 57.

Jerusha, born September 18th, 1775 ; died March 31st, 1863 ; married Ira Gates.

Mary, died in infancy ; Mary 2, married George Little, of Pennsylvania ; she died September 13th, 1836. They had four sons, who are lawyers, prominent in their profession and well off. One resides in Tunkhannock, Pa.; one in Towanda ; one in Montrose, and one in Bloomsburg. They all have sons who are lawyers.

Annie married Ambrose Niles about 1780.

Children : Wm. H., founder of the *Sentinel and Witness* of Middletown. He and his three children are dead. His widow, aged 84, lives with the writer at Whitestone, N. Y. Col. Aaron Tarbox Niles married Rachel Ann Harris, of Millington. Had five children. All the family except the writer died many years ago.

Annie Estabrook Niles married second, John Markham, of Chatham, in 1812. She died in 1849, aged 71. He died in 1852, aged 96. Their descendants mostly live in Chatham.

Olive Estabrook died young.

Hobert 3, born May 9th, 1787, married Ascenath Harvey, of Millington. In November, 1827, he was appointed Commissioner of Lands, 16,000 acres belonging to the Connecticut School Fund, and moved to Newfield, N. Y. He died at Havana in 1872. Children : Robert, resides at Newfield. His children live near by. Rhoda married a Rockwell ; Mary, an Alexander ; Isaac, a Smith ; Clara, an Allen ; Addie is unmarried and lives at home.

George, son of Hobert, lives at Andover ; Herman lives at Ithaca ; has one son, William.

CHAPTER IX.

MILLINGTON CONGREGATIONAL CHURCH.

The first meeting house was erected in Millington in 1743. It was fifty by forty feet, and stood on the Green, a few rods south of the present church. The building of the present house was proposed in Society meeting, January 21st, 1832, when it was " voted that the Society build a meeting house 32 feet by 44, from 16 to 18 feet posts, with a steeple not exceeding 60 feet in height." The house was built by Mr. Edward Worthington and dedicated to divine service on the 23d of January, 1833. The Society tendered Mr. Worthington a vote of thanks for faithful discharge of his work. For the excellent bell on the church the Society were mainly indebted to John Chapman and William H. Cone—to the former for his liberal subscription ; to the latter for his great activity in the matter.

The first minister in Millington was Rev. Timothy Symmes, of Scituate, Mass., who was ordained December 2d, 1736. Dr. Field says : " In the great revival of religion which spread in New England a few years after his ordination, his feelings were extravagantly raised, and he prosecuted his work with a zeal not according to his knowledge. This gave rise to difficulties which ended in his dismission in 1743."

He was succeeded by Mr. Hobart Esterbrook, son of the Rev. Mr. Esterbrook, of Canterbury. He graduated at New Haven in 1736, and was ordained in Millington, November 20th, 1745. He was a steady, judicious and faithful minister, and is remembered with respect and affection by his people. He died January 28th, 1766, in the 50th year of his age and 20th of his ministry. (For a record of their descendants see chapter eight.) His first wife was Miss Hannah Williams, of Mansfield, by whom he had two daughters, who died young. His second wife was Jerusha Chauncey, daughter of the Rev. Isaac Chauncey, of Hadley, Mass., by whom he had four children. She died June 17th, 1776, aged 62 years, and was buried beside her husband in Millington burying ground.

The next minister in Millington was Mr. Diodate Johnson, who was ordained July 2d, 1767. He was a son of the Rev. Stephen Johnson, of Lyme, was educated at Yale College, where he took his first degree in 1764, and became a tutor. Endowed with superior genius and learning, and animated with fervent zeal for his work, he entered the ministry with the fairest prospects of usefulness. His labors, however, was soon ended, for consumption closed his life January 15th, 1773, at the early age of 28. He was sitting in his chair reading an article in " Doddrige's Rise and Progress," entitled " A Meditation and Prayer suited to the Case of a Dying Christian," when struck with death.

Rev. Eleazer Sweetland was installed May 21st, 1777. He was a native of Hebron, and graduated at Dartmouth College, in 1774. He died March 25th, 1787, aged 36 years, much beloved and respected by all who knew him. He left a wife and three children, who moved soon after from Millington.

Rev. William Lyman, D. D., was ordained December 13th, 1787. He maintained his pastoral relation with the church at Millington for thirty-five years, and was known as one of the most popular and eloquent preachers in this part of the country. He had a powerful voice, an easy flow of words, and all his writings were stamped with vigor and power. In the latter part of his ministry he became afflicted with hypochondria. This, with his independent manner, finally aroused an opposition among his people, and at a society meeting held on the 23d of May, 1822, it was voted " that a committee of five be appointed to consult the interests of the society, especially as it respects our relations with Dr. Lyman as our minister." William Cone, Esq., Deacon N. B. Beckwith, Deacon Israel Cone, Russel Dutton, Esq., and Captain Hobart Esterbrook, were appointed as said committee. The committee reported against the Doctor, and on the last Wednesday in August, at a meeting of the Ecclesiastical Council, the relation between pastor and people was dissolved. His farewell sermon, replete with denunciations of the sins and shortcomings of his flock, was delivered with such vigor and eloquence that the long years which have intervened have failed to obliterate its impressions from the minds of those who heard him, and his hymn about the conspiracy of " wicked men" was in keeping with his sermon.   Many anecdotes are related of Dr. Lyman's dry humor and eccentricity, which he often carried to the pulpit.

In his day the temperance agitation had scarcely commenced, and the indulgence of the social glass among the higher class was much more common than now.   The clergy and the elders were wont to meet and discuss grave matters over their toddy with a freedom that would be quite scandalous in these days.   Mr. Elijah Parsons used to call regularly upon an old lady of the same name who lived where Charles Babcock now resides in the Landing and get his mug of " flip."   The old lady, knowing his hours, used to have her " flip-iron" hot, and concoct his favorite beverage with dexterity and skill.   Dr. Lyman and Rev. Mr. Vail, of Hadlyme, who were his cotemporaries, were wont, at regular intervals to meet him at the " Blacksmith's Arms," (the house north of Maplewood Seminary), and discuss grave matters belonging to their profession over their " mugs of flip."   So, too, in those days, the General Assembly used to open with an election sermon, which furnished an occasion for a general gathering of the clergy throughout the State. Great dinners were furnished at the expense of the State, and "Santa Cruz" was a prominent feature of the bill of fare. It is related of Dr. Lyman that at an Ecclesiastical Council held in Westchester, when the company, being invited to refresh them selves at the sideboard, one of his ministerial brethren suggested that their *first* refreshment should be to wash off the dust of travel, the Doctor decided the matter by the following epigram :

Our fathers of old
First washed their eyes,
And then their throats ;
But we, their sons, more wise,
Will wash our throats,
And *then* our eyes.

One day, being met on the street by a friend, he was accosted with :

" Good morning, Doctor ; what is the news ?"

" There is great news," replied the Doctor ; " I just saw a man up here at Boardman's store swallowing a dozen ax-helves !"

" I declare! how did he do it ?"

" Why, it seems very easy ; he had traded his helves for liquor, and when I left he had poured nearly all of them down his throat."

At a time of great drought the Doctor arose in his pulpit one morning and prayed for rain in this wise : " Oh, Lord, we pray Thee to send down copious and refreshing showers, that the parched earth may revive and bring forth grass—*for geese!*"

Dr. Lyman moved to Western New York, where he died several years ago. Soon after his dismission a wonderful revival of religion occurred in

Millington, under the ministry of the Rev. Mr. Saxon, called to this day by the good people of Millington " The Great Revival."

Dr. Lyman was succeeded by the Rev. Hermon Yail, who was ordained April 6th, 1825. In September, 1827, Mr. Vail asked for a dismission from his pastoral charge, which was granted by the Ecclesiastical Council soon after. For nearly three years afterwards the society was without any regular pastor. In 1830, the Rev. Nathaniel Miner received a call from the society, which he declined, principally on account of the dilapidated condition of the old meeting house. He occupied the pulpit, however, as a stated supply for three years, and was installed as their regalar pastor May 28th, 1833, which was after the erection and dedication of the new meeting house.

Mr. Miner was born in Stonington, Connecticut, educated at the " Literary and Theological Seminary" of Bangor, Maine, and received the honorary degree of Master of Arts from Amherst College in 1840. He was ordained at Chesterfield (Montville), October, 1826 ; went to Millington from Bozrahville in 1830. His salary was at first $375, then $450, and finally $500 per year. Near the close of his ministry in Millington a small farm was purchased, formerly owned by Rev. Hobart Esterbrook, and on it was erected what is now known as the Millington parsonage.

Mr. Miner married Emeline S. Ransom, of Salem, by whom he had five children. Three of them are living, "two are not and yet are." He was dismissed from his pastoral charge in Millington at his own request by the Middlesex Consociation at their annual meeting held at Essex, October, 1858. Since that time he has resided in Salem, and has retired from active service.

Mr. Miner occupies a large space in the affectionate remembrance of his parishioners. As a minister, he was ever earnestly devoted to the service of his Master, and the welfare of his flock ; as a neighbor, his genial kindness, his sociability, and the hospitality of his home made his religion a practical reality instead of an abstract theory. For the young (and in this relation the writer's recollection of him will always add pleasure to memory,) he ever had a kind word and a helping hand, which wielded an influence for good.

Mr. Miner was succeeded by Rev. A. C. Beach, from Wolcot, Conn. He was born at Orange, N. J.; a graduate of Yale College, in 1835, and was installed as pastor of the church in Millington in 1859. He was dismissed in 1876, and was succeeded by the Rev. Mr. Griswold, who is still in charge.

The deacons of the Congregational Church in Millington since its organization have been as follows ·

Name.	Elected.	Died.	Age.
Samuel Emmons,	Oct., 1736	————	—
Daniel Gates,	Oct., 1736	————	—
Gen. Jos. Spencer,	Nov. 20, 1767	Jan. 13, 1789	75
Samuel Dutton,	July 4, 1771	Dec. 30, 1790	87

Name.	Elected.	Died.	Age.
Ebenezer Dutton,	Feb. 26, 1778	Moved to Lebanon	
Benjamin Fuller	Feb. 26, 1778	Nov. 10, 1815	93
Nathaniel Cone,	May, 1789	Apr. 15, 1790	78
Barzillail Beckwith,	June 4, 1790	Feb. 22, 1818	79
Isaac Spencer	April 1, 1796	———————	—
Diodate Lord,	Aug. 26, 1816	Moved away.	
Israel Cone, Jr.,	April 17, 1818	———————	—
Nathaniel Beckwith,	April 17, 1818	1858	
Wm. E. Cone,	Moved to Moodus.	Deacon in 1st Congregational Church.	
Samuel Arnold,	April 30, 1841	Now in office.	
Epaphroditus Gates,	Aug. 27, 1858		
Charles Miner,		Now in office.	

CHAPTER X.

HADLYME.—HUNGERFORD AND WILLEY FAMILIES.

The Society of Hadlyme was formed from East Haddam Society, and Lyme Third Society, in October, 1742. About two-thirds of the Society is in East Haddam. The meeting house was erected soon after. The church was organized with ten male members on the 20th of June 1745, at the house of Lieut. John Comstock, and on the 18th of September following the Rev. Grindal Rawson was installed its pastor. Here is a copy of the original record :

" Att a General Assembly holden att New Haven, on the 14th Day of October Ano: dom—1742— Upon the memorial of Isaac Willey, Stephen Scovil, John Comstock and other members of the first Society in East Haddam and the third Society in Lyme prefered to this Assembly in May Last and the Report of the Comitte thereon—to this Assembly in their present Sessions proposing that ye memorials : st be formed into a Distinct Society for Carrying on ye worship of God a-mongst themselves according to ye Bounds &c—Limits therein Specified. This Assembly Do Enact Decree and Order That ye said Isaac Willey, Stephen Scovil, John Comstock and the Rest of the Inhabitants of the Parrish hereafter Described be and they are here by Imbodyed and made one Distinct Ecclesiastical Society by the name of Hadlyme, and that ye Bounds thereof to be as follows viz Beginning at a Whiteoak Tree Standing by the Great River being accounted ye bounds between Lyme and East Haddam thence Running Southerly to William Clemans In cluding Mr. Selden's farm by the River thence Eastward from said Clemans house unto ye house where Consider Tiffany now lives including that house thence running northwesterly to the South East corner of James Masses farm thence Running northeasterly by s'd Masses his Land to the Repouted bounds of East Haddam. Then beginning at s'd Whiteoak Tree by the River from thence Extending one mile and three quarters north To the River and from the Extreem of that Extent Easterly to James Booge's house including s'd house thence Easterly to Elijah Ackley's house including s'd House thence East unto the Line of Millington Parrish and from thence Southerly By s'd Millington Line unto the Line between s'd East Haddam and Lyme and by Last mentioned Line unto Mose his Land aforesaid.

Teste George Wyllys, Secretary."

At a meeting held " May ye 28, 1745 it was then and their voted that wee Will Give ye Rev. Mr. Rawson towards building his house in s'd society if he Settles in the work of the ministre a-mongst us the sum of one hundred pound old tenor in Labour to be payd in the time that we way his settlement."

Mr. Rawson was born at Mendon, Mass.; received the degree of A. B., at Harvard in 1728, and was settled several years at South Hadley. He was a plain preacher, gifted in prayer, remarkably social, and had an uncommon talent in reconciling parties at variance. He died March 29, 1777, in the 70th year of his age and the 22d of his ministry in Hadlyme. His wife was Dorothy Chauncey, daughter of the Rev. Isaac Chauncey, of Hadley. She died November 15th, 1870, aged 70 years. They had seven children, all of whom, with one exception, died before their parents The Hadlyme parsonage—the large brown house on the hill now occupied by E. W. Mather—was built about 1746. Mr. Rawson lived here during his ministry. Afterwards his son, Rev. E. G. Rawson, brought up a large family—in fact, for over one hundred years it was the home of the ministers.

The Rev. Joseph Vail succeeded Mr. Rawson, and was installed February 9th, 1780. He retained his pastoral charge more than fifty years. He was succeeded by Rev. R. S. Crompton about 1835. Mr. Crompton was secceeded by Rev. George Carrington, S. A. Loper, E. B. Hilliard, D. W. Zeller. The following notice was cut from the *Conn. Val. Advertiser* in 1885 :

"Rev. Stephen A. Loper, of Hadlyme, died in Hartford, on Friday of last week, at the ripe age of 84 years and six months. Nearly a half century ago Mr. Loper was the pastor of the Congregational church at Middle Haddam, after which he was for many years pastor of the Congregational Church in Hadlyme. For several years past he has lived with his daughter, Mrs. Lynde Selden, at the last-named place."

The deacons in the church since its organization were ·

Samuel Dutton,	Christopher Holmes,
Samuel Cooby,	Col. Samuel Selden,
Israel Spencer, Esq.,	Jabez Comstock,
Israel S. Spencer,	Israel Dewey,
Ithamer Harvey,	Selden Warren,
Elijah Comstock,	Samuel C. Selden,
F. A. Tiffany,	Isaac Chester,
Joseph Selden,	William C. Spencer.
Almond Day,	

Notwithstanding the formation of this society was nine years after the formation of Millington, settlements were made here much earlier, or about the time of the settlement of the Creek Row.

Thomas Hungerford moved to this parish from New London, with his three sons, as early as 1692. He was soon followed by Isaac Willey and his three sons, also from New London. John Holmes moved here from the same place in 1710, and Thomas Harvey from England, and John Marsh from Massachusetts were also early inhabitants. The Hungerfords, Willeys and Holmes seem to have taken firm root in the soil, as their descendants are now quite numerous here, and " own and possess " a large portion of the land. Thomas

Hungerford was a blacksmith, and in consideration
of his trade the society of East Haddam gave him
a section of land. His house stood at the corner
of the road east of Asa Hungerford's, near the Old
Bone Mill. He was the first selectman of the town
of East Haddam. He died about 1714, and was
buried in the Cove Burying Ground. The three
sons who accompanied him hither were named
Thomas, John and Green. At that time Thomas
2d was married, and had one child. Later he was
a sea-faring man, and when at home, lived with
and took care of his father. On his return from his
last voyage at sea, he was taken sick at New London, where he died in 1750. His descendants
left town. John, the second son of the elder
Thomas, married Deborah Spencer about 1701.
He died in 1748, and was buried in Hadlyme burying ground. He had two sons, Robert and Thomas.
Robert built a house which stood where Drury
Holmes now lives, in which he resided till his
death. He married Grace Holmes about 1730.
His children were Robert, John, Zackariah, Elijah,
Deborah, Anna and Silence.

Robert 2d married in 1776. His children by his
second wife were as follows ·

Robert 3d, born in 1777.

Joseph E., born in 1784,

William, born in 1786.

Lovica, born in 1789.

Ansel 1st, born in 1792.

Asa, born in 1795.

Richard, born in 1798,

Ansel 2d born in———.

Rebecca, born in 1804.

Ansel 1st died about the year 1800. Richard was killed by a falling tree in 1815. Ansel 2d and Rebecca Ely are now living in Hadlyme.

John, the brother of Robert 2d, served in the French and Indian wars. Captain Zackariah married Lydia Bigelow, and built the house where William E. now lives; he was grandfather of William E., Zachariah 3d, John B. Hungerford and Roswell S. Cone, our present townsmen.

Green Hungerford, the son of the elder Thomas, moved to Millington about 1730, where he became one of the leading men of the society.

He married Jemima Richardson, and built a house at 'Tator Hill, where Norris Rathburn's house now stands. He had a son Green, who occupied the old homestead, which subsequently became used as a public house, and the headquarters of the militia for a number of years. The widow of Green married Matthias Fuller, the father of Richardson Fuller. The grandchildren of Green 2d are Reed Anderson, Lord W. Cone's mother, Richard Hungerford's mother, and Mrs. Olcot Harris.

Isaac Willey came from New London with Thomas Hungerford, and also settled in Hadlyme with his three sons, Isaac, John and Abel. They owned land from the Connecticut river, extending back several miles along the line of the town of Lyme.

All the Willeys in East Haddam are descendants from this family, though they are not now as numerous as formerly, many of them having moved from the town.

Abel settled in the southern part of Hadlyme, upon the old homestead.

John's children were named Joseph, Jonathan and Allen. Joseph 2d married Irene Banning in 1764. Their child, Temperance born 1768. Jonathan married Mary Bates in 1758. Their children were :

Susanna, born in 1758.

Mary, born in 1761

Jonathan 2d, born in 1763.

Clement, born in 1765.

Azubah, born in 1767.

Elles, born in 1769.

Hannah, born in 1771.

Keziah, born in 1773.

The children of Allen were Abraham, John and Judah.

Captain Abraham married Susanna Beckwith in 1773. Their children were :

Anna, born in 1773.

Ethan Allen, born in 1776.

Mehitable R., born in 1780.

Barak born in 1782.

Susanna, born in 1785.

Abraham Wolcott born in 1788.

Ethan Allen Willey was the father of Judge Willey, William Willey and Mrs. Orren Warner, of East Haddam. Mehitable R., the sister of Ethan Allen, married a Chapman, and was the mother of Robert W. Chapman, Esq.

CHAPTER XI.

LEESVILLE.

One of the first settlers of Leesville was Capt. Jonathan Kilburn, whose house stood on the hill, near the present schoolhouse. The Captain was a man of considerable influence in his day. He seems to have been enterprising, eccentric, and ingenious. The mill-house near the present Leesville dam stands over what was then called "Salmon Hole," a deep hole from which were caught large numbers of salmon. The large chasm in the ledge, just east of this house, is a monument of Capt. Kilburn's perseverance, he having burned it out by the use of fire and water. He then built a trough from a spring on the hill some distance east of the village to the bank which towered above the present school-house, and by thus washing away this mountain of sand and sending it through the chasm, filled up "Salmon Hole," and made the fertile garden spot around the old mill house. Afterwards he erected a dam across the river where the present dam is, and about the year 1765 built an oil mill, the first in the State, near where the present cotton mill stands.

In his old age, Capt. Kilburn became considerably involved, his principal creditors being the Lords, who were, for those times, wealthy merchants, living at the Landing, and to whom fickle fortune transferred the old man's property. George Lord lived where Richard Gelston now resides, Samuel Lord built the brick hotel which subsequently became the Champion House. George and Richard Lord moved to Leesville, and through their energy and means this splendid water privilege became partially developed. Over the oil mill they erected a woolen factory and a clothier's works, where they fulled and dressed their cloth. They also had a bark mill, and erected a saw mill, carrying eight saws, and sawing a length of seventy feet. The woolen mill had five spinning machines, and consumed about ten thousand pounds of wool annually. The place arose to the dignity of a name, and was called Lord's Mills. A cotton factory was next erected at the same spot.

On the night of the 30th of March, 1815, these mills, with a large portion of their contents, were consumed by fire, occasioning a loss of about twenty-five thousand dollars. The origin of the fire was never ascertained, but from some circumstances which subsequently came to light, suspicions were directed to the crew of a British vessel which lay near the mouth of the river, the English being at that time bitterly opposed to American manufactures, then in their infancy.

Notwithstanding this heavy loss, the Lords, the summer after, erected a fine brick building, 65x35, four stories high, with a loft in the garret. Into this they introduced machinery for the manufacture of woolen cloth, using sixteen thousand pounds of wool a year.

In 1816, they introduced five hundred cotton spindles, which they afterwards increased to two thousand. They also had in this building a machine room, where all the wood, brass, and iron machinery were made and repaired for the establishment.

Fortune's wheel finally turned disastrously for the Lords. Owing to severe losses they were forced to mortgage their property heavily to the State of Connecticut, and a foreclosure was the result. The place was purchased by the sons of Dr. Samuel H. B. Lee, of New London, who gave to it the name which it still retains. The Lees afterwards sold the mills to Enoch and Samuel Parsons. Soon afterwards a company was formed, consisting of Parsons, Chapman, D. B. Warner, and S. S. Card. After holding the property about eight years, they sold it to Ackley Cowdrey, through whose agency a joint stock company was formed.

About twenty-two years ago, the new mill was destroyed by fire, and on the ruins was erected the present mill, which is owned by the East Haddam Duck Company, and run for the manufacture of cotton duck. It uses about two hundred thousand pounds of cotton per year.

The Lords went from Leesville to New Connectient, which they purchased. It appears that at one time Richard and George became so disastrously involved by their losses at Leesville that they were sent to jail for debt.   Three of the daughters married Burroughs, one of them a Member of Con gress.   Samuel went to Spain and brought a load of gold, as he called it, to this country.   The ore upon being assayed did not prove to be the genuine article, yet the cargo was found not entirely worthless.   It brought considerable money, but a fraction, however, of what its owners anticipated.

Of the Kilburn family, Jonathan 2d went to Killingworth.   Jonathan 3d is now in Middletown; owns the Farmers' and Mechanics' Hotel.   Aaron worked for some time in a silversmith's shop, run by one Wm. Johnson.   He now resides in New Haven.

The original Capt. Kilburn left another enduring monument to his memory in the shape of a large stone basin, capable of holding two or three barrels of water, which now stands as it has stood for years in front of the old Kilburn House.   Capt. K. dug out this solid rock, placed it there as a reservoir, drilled a hole through the bottom, and connected it with the spring on the hill by a wooden pipe composed of bored logs.   Into this cool res ervoir for many years there bubbled up a spring of pure cold water, affording a convenience and a comfort which our farmers of the present day seldom enjoy.

The Leesville of to-day is a pleasant village of about fifteen families, the heads of which are worthy citizens, noted for honesty, frugality, and— Democracy.

During all the Republican administrations of the past twenty-five years, it has had to depend on a democratic post-master or close the office.

The large house in the centre of the village—also a centre of hospitality—has for many years been occupied by Mr. Charles Wright and his stalwart sons.. John A. Wright kept a store here for many years. At present (1886), he is located at Thorndyke, Mass., and has recently been appointed post-master at that place.

CHAPTER XII.

BAPTIST, METHODIST AMD EPISCOPAL CHURCHES.

The Baptist Church in East Haddam was originally " The Third Baptist Church in Colchester."
The Church was organized at the house of David
Miner, November 22d, 1809. The first meeting
was held at Bulkley Hill school house December
15th, 1809—preaching by Elder Eliada Blakesley.
Among the familiar names of the early members
are John and Guy Bigelow, Daniel Bulkley, Anson
Ackley, Seth Hayes and Turner Miner. The
church prospered and increased in numbers notwithstanding they had no regular place of worship,
services being held in the school house and occa
sionally at the house of some member for sixteen
years. The first meeting in East Haddam was held
at the school house in the northwest district December 22d, 1825. Soon after, on the 15th of December, the first meeting was held in their new
meeting house on the East Haddam and Colchester Turnpike, where Ransom Rathburn now lives.
About this time the name was changed to " The
Baptist Church of Colchester and East Haddam."
The first sermon in the new meeting house was
preached by Elder Stanwood, from the text : " One
thing have I desired of the Lord, and that will I

seek after, that I might dwell in the house of the Lord." Changes in place of worship, and the erection of new meeting houses are not generally productive of harmony in any denomination. It seems that this change was no exception to the general rule, for cases of discipline, for contempt against some of the most prominent members, became quite frequent soon after the removal. In fact, during the fifty years that have elapsed since that time this society has been particularly prominent in its intestine strifes. The last strife, but a year or two since, wherein the Beebe faction was arrayed against the Brooks and Stark faction in the civil and ecclesiastical courts. Injunctions and counter injunctions, more potent than the Pope's bulls, closing the doors of the church for months ; a fight which was widely known and discussed as the " Moodus Church war," is fresh in the memory of every townsman. The first pastor of the new church was Alvin Ackley, June 19th 1827. June 18th, 1833, Amos Watrous, and on September 3d, 1845, Thomas N. Dickinson were set apart as preachers of the Word. August 1st, 1844, it was voted to sell the meeting house in Millington, and put the avails in a building for public worship in Mechanicsville (Moodus). On the 21st of September following, the church was organized, under the name of the " Central Baptist Church in East Haddam." New articles of faith were adopted, and since that time the place of worship has been at their new house in Moodus.

The first pastor of the church in Moodus was Elder Bela Hicks, whose successors have been as follows ·

Rev. A. J. Watrous, Elder Knapp, Levi Wakeman.
June 18th, 1854—Elder James M. Phillips.
August 31st, 1856—Elder A. Watrous.
May 3d, 1858—Rev. A. V. Dimmock.
September 6th, 1862—Rev. Mr. Haven.
March 25th, 1866—Rev. Thomas Attwood.
April 30th, 1867—Rev. Percival Matthewson.
May 8th, 1870—Rev. C. N. Nichols.

The present parsonage was purchased in 1868 for two thousand dollars.

" The M. E. Church of the Mechanicsville Station " was organized, and the church erected upon its present site about 1834. It is under the control of the Providence Conference. The Presiding Elders of the district have been as follows ·

Daniel Dorchester,	1835–37	Erastus Burton,	1860–62
Asa U. Swinerton,	1838–41	George U. Carpenter,	
William Livesey,	1842		1863–64
Ralph W. Allen,	1843–46	Parden T. Keeney,	1865–69
Erastus Benton,	1847–50	George W. Brewster,	1870
Bartholomew Otherman,		H. S. Smith,	1870–73
	1851–54	Anthony Palmer,	1873–74
Levi Daggett,	1855–56	James H. Nutting,	1874–77
Anthony Palmer,	1857–58	A. W. Paige,	1877–78
L. W. Blood,	1859–60	A. E. Anthony,	1878

The following is the list of preachers ·

Freeman Nutting,	1835	Warren Emerson,	1853–54
Amos Simpson,	1835	J. F. Sheffield,	1855
David Todd,	1836–37	N. Goodrich,	1858–59

John F. Blanchard, 1837
James Nichols, 1838
Solomon Cushman, 1838
Theodore W. Gile, 1839
Charles C. Barnes, 1841
Moses Stoddard, 1841
William Simmons, 1846
B. L. Sayer. 1847
Henry Torbush, 1849
Geo. W. Brewster, 1850
R. Albiston, 1851-52

H. W. Conant, 1860
—— Burnham, 1860
L. D. Bentley, 1861
C. M. Alvord, 1862-63
F. H. Brown, 1864
G. W. Wooding, 1865-67
Joel B. Bishop, 1868
William Turkinton, 1868-69
J. N. Worcester, 1870
H. S. Smith, 1871

The Episcopal Society was formed April 27th, 1791, in consequence of a division among the people of the First Congregational Society respecting the location of their present meeting house. In 1792 the Rev. Solomon Blakeley was placed over the Society as deacon, and a year later was placed in full orders. He labored with this and neighboring societies for more than twenty years. He moved to St. James Church, New London, in 1815. Returned, and again became rector from 1818 to October 8th, 1821. The rectors who succeeded him were as follows :

Rev. Seth Paddock, during part of the year 1822.

Rev. William James, from October 8th, 1822, until January 29th, 1827.

Rev. Peter G. Clark, two-thirds of the time from November 8th, 1827, until May, 1833.

Rev. Stephen Beach, from June 20th 1833, until his death, January 14th, 1838.

Rev. William G. Hyes, from June, 1838, until November 1st, 1838.

Rev. Charles W. Bradley, from February 10th, 1839, until August 2d, 1840.

Rev. Albert G. Isaacs, (deacon) from August to November, 1840.

Rev. Thomas G. Salter, from March 21st, 1841, until November 21st, 1842.

Rev. Alex. Burgen (deacon), from November 28th, 1842, until December 11th, 1842.

Rev. Henry DeKoven (deacon), was appointed minister October 29th, 1843, and resigned September 1st, 1844.

Rev. Alpheus Geer, from September 1st, 1844, until April 12th, 1852.

Rev. George W. Nichols, from May 19th, 1852, until April 12th, 1853. Again, from July 2d, 1854, until September 30th, 1855.

Rev. B. F. Taylor, from December, 1853, to July, 1854.

Rev. Gilbert B. Hayden, from September 30th, 1855, until September 17th, 1856.

Rev. Michael Scofield, from September to November, 1856.

Rev. H. B. Hitchings (deacon), from 1857, until November 1st, 1862.

Rev. Henry T. Gregory, from November, 1862, until April 13th, 1868. During his pastorate the present parsonage was built.

Rev. E. C. Gardner, from October, 1868, until 1872.

Rev. George Rumsey, from February 7th, 1872, until October, 1884.

Rev. A. T. Parsons succeeded Mr. Rumsey, and is still in charge (1886). He is a graduate of Trinity College and Berkley Divinity School.

Inscription on the bell of St. Stephens Church

" Ano de 815,
Serudo Prion E. I. V.
P. Du Miguel Villa
Mueva Procunador,
El V. Du Josef
Estavana. A. D. 815.

Som do, Prion E. J. V. P. Du Miguel Villa
Mueva Procunador, Elv. Du Josef Estavano."

TRANSLATION.

The Prior, being the most Rev. Father Miguel Villa Mueva, The Procurator, the most Rev. Father Jose F. Estevan-Corvalis has made me. Made in the year A. D. 815.

It hung many years in a Spanish Monastery, and was taken down during the wars of Napoleon I. It is said to be the oldest bell in the United States.

CHAPTER XIII.

CEMETERIES.

For many years after the settlement of the town the people carried their dead across the river to Haddam for burial. Not far from the year 1700, a party of mourners, bearing their dead, crossed the Cove and the narrow peninsula of Haddam Neck, and attempted to cross the river. It had overflowed its banks and the floating ice rendered a passage impossible. Slowly and sadly the procession retraced its steps through the snow, and buried its dead in the forest in a romantic spot a little back from the Cove. This person was Mrs. Arnold, a great, great aunt of Mrs. Elijah Bingham. Thus commenced the Cove burial ground, and the place is now known as "Grave Yard Point." It is situated about one and a half miles north of the Landing, and a little west of William O. Brainerd's. Although the spot has twice been cleared of wood within ninety years, large trees stand beside the rude grave stones as if to offer their protection, and throw over the spot their solemn shade. The brown stones, covered with the moss of time, are adorned by the traditional angels having the usual round heads with wings protruding from the ears. In a prominent part of the cemetery is a moss-covered tabular monument with

this inscription: "Under this tombstone lyeth in-
terred the body of the Rev. Stephen Hosmer, the
first Pastor of the First Church of Christ in East
Haddam, who departed this life the 18th day of
June, A. D., 1749, and in the 70th year of his age.
And at his right hand lyeth Mrs. Sarah Hosmer,
his beloved consort, who departed this life September ye 30th, A. D. 1749, and in the 67th year of her
age.

> "Sweet souls we leave you to your rest,
> Enjoy your Jesus and your God,
> Till we from bands of clay released,
> Spring out and climb the shining road."

Near this is another slab of brown stone with
this inscription· "Here lieth the body of Thomas
Gates, Justice of the Peace, April ye 20th, 1734,
in ye 70th year of his age." Also, another slab
recording the death of Dea. Daniel Brainerd,
who died 1743." Beside this stands a handsome
stone for those days, which has remained in a good
state of preservation, and records the death of
Capt. Joshua Brainard, who departed this life May
the 13th, A. D. 1755, in the 84th year of his age."
In a line with this, stand rude brown stones which
mark the graves of Nehimiah, Lucy, Uri and Hannah Brainard, and at the end of the line stands the
only marble stones in the yard. They mark the
graves of Bezaliel Brainard and Lydia his wife.
They were the grandparents of Wm. O. and Abby
Brainard who own the ground. Here, too, is the
resting place of the Cones, the Ackleys, Arnolds,

Olmsteads and many old families of the town. A more pleasant or romantic spot than this can hardly be found. Moodus and the Landings, instead of each having a cemetery, should have united and purchased this spot for a common burial ground. The distance from either place is convenient. Nature, history and tradition have already made it an interesting spot; it would only have needed the embellishments of art, to make it a retreat of which the town might well be proud. One cannot wander through this silent city of the dead, without his mind reverting to the time, when its occupants roamed over these hills and possessed our present homes. Their rude boats were moored beside the ruder canoes of the Indians in the snug harbor afforded by the Cove, or glided in friendly rivalry over the peaceful waters of the Connecticut. But one generation removed from their Puritan fathers, they inherited their virtues and their faith, and were loyal subjects of their God and King. At last, weary with life's toils they laid down to sleep beneath these pleasant shades, and for nearly two centuries the din and confusion of progress and civilization have failed to disturb their silent repose. The mourner who was wont to visit this retreat with a secret yet melancholy pleasure comes now no more. The flowers and shrubs which once fringed these lowly graves, and which the hand of friendship delighted to cherish, are replaced by those of Nature's own bestowing, for God has not forgotten them. "He sends the golden beams of

the morning to shine upon the tree-tops with refreshing cheerfulness, and the lingering tints of
evening to hover over them with a tranquilizing
glow." The other grave yards in East Haddam
were laid out or commenced as follows:

Old Yard in Hadlyme, 1723.
Long Pond Yard, 1726.
Moodus Yard, 1748.
Meeting House Yard in Hadlyme, 1750.
Bashan, 1760.
'Tater Hill, 1760.
Near Millington Green, 1764.
Eight Mile River, 1769.
Landing, 1773.
Mt. Parnassus, 1774.
Centre Cong. Church, 1778.
Wicket Lane, 1793.

There is probably no more healthy town in the
State, the air and water being uncommonly pure.
Some of the old accounts refer to periods when
virulent diseases prevailed throughout the town,
but of nothing very serious. Within a few years
past, malaria has prevailed, to some extent, along
the river, and in fact it has prevailed throughout
the whole State. In the year 1775, there were over
forty deaths in the town ; in the year following,
more than fifty. The population of East Haddam,
in 1800, was 2,805. The total number of deaths in
the town for ten years after was 614, or an average
of over sixty each year, being a much larger aver-

age of mortality than has existed since that time.
In 1870, the population was but 2,952, or 147 more
than it was at the beginning of the century. The
number of deaths during the year ending June 1st,
1870, was 5.4, or an average of 1 in 55 persons.
Twenty of those deaths were caused by consumption, six from typhoid fever, two were accidental.
The other deaths resulted from diseases pertaining
to childhood and old age. Twenty-two of the
number were under twenty-three years of age;
eleven over seventy; seven over eighty, and one
over ninety years. Thus while two-fifths failed to
reach the average of human life, more than one-
third passed the three-score years and ten alloted
to man by the Creator.

CHAPTER XIV.

ACKLEY—PALMES—HARRIS—MARTIN.

The old road running east from the Col. Orrin Warner farm was formerly a main thoroughfare, and on it lived several of the old families. On the spot where Henry Martin now lives were raised three generations of Ackleys. Three brothers by the name of Ackley came over from England about 1740. Elijah built the house where Abby Ann now lives solitary and alone, over one hundred and thirty-five years ago. It has always remained in the family. Alvin Ackley died there about twenty-five years ago, aged eighty-five. Several members of the family moved West. Julius Ackley died here recently. The farm originally extended up to the Wicket Lane School House. Enoch and Jeremiah Ackley came from Chatham. The latter acquired a comfortable home at Goodspeeds, and has been one of Boardman's managers for many years. Enoch bought the Alfred Gates place, half-way between the two landings, and moved there about 1867. He was an eccentric and withal a popular character. He lived with great frugality and appeared to be working hard to get out of debt. He was a regular man-of-all-work for the neighborhood. If a man wanted some coal shoveled in, snow paths made, or a ditch dug ; if a housewife wanted her carpets shaken, or her rooms whitewashed, Enoch was the man to do it. When he could not get a job he played checkers. If he had invented a family coat-of-arms it would probably have been a shovel and whitewash brush engraved on a checker-board, with a rooster for the crest. He was without personal pride, yet he was proud of his four pretty daughters, and they were popular girls. He was genial, obliging and well liked—but "poor" When he died, three years ago, he was found to be worth about one hundred and twenty-five thousand dollars!

The house now owned by Christopher Brockway was called the Samuel Palmes' place—Palmes died there at the age of ninety-five. His son Guy, the father of Oliver, John and Sarah, died recently at the residence of his daughter, in Colchester, having reached nearly one hundred years. The family is of Scotch descent, its ancestors in this country having first settled in New London. Samuel was a tanner, and when a young man, worked and learned his trade at a tannery on the farm known as "Palmes Place" The old vats still exist. He subsequently built a tannery and dwelling house on the river road just north of Shailor Cone's. Just below Abby Ann Ackley's is an old chimney where once lived Joe Warner, who was the grandfather of Joseph Warner of Hadlyme. Running east from the Ackley farm is an old road known as Pike's Lane. On this road lived one Thomas Riley, who, in his younger days, according to tradition, sailed over the seas with Capt. Robert Kidd. Farther east, on the road leading from Mt. Parnassus to Hadlyme, is the old Parker homestead, now owned and occupied by Ozias Parker, the youngest son of a large family. His brothers all left the town in their early days to seek their fortunes, and were very successful. John lives in Madison, Conn.; has one son. Elial lives in Deep River. Avery is a jeweler in Flemington, N. J.; he has two daughters and one son. His oldest daughter married Henry A. Fluck, a popular lawyer of Flemington. Acenath, their only sister, married Aaron T. Niles, and after his death married Russell Babcock, of North Lyme. She is now a widow. Ozias has several times represented the town in the State Legislature, and has worthily filled the most important town offices. His oldest son, Francis, graduated at Wesleyan University, and is now a promising lawyer in Hartford.

Further north, on the same street, are remains of the homestead of the Andrews family. The owner of the farm moved about the year 1810 to Ohio, which was then considered the far West. His nephew become a popular and eloquent preacher of the Congregational faith, and about the year 1870 was called to the charge of the first Congregational Church in East Hampton, Conn.

HARRIS.

In an old red house on the Ripley Tracy farm on Mt. Parnassus, lived Samuel Harris, who moved

there from Salem early in the present century.
Selden Harris, of Montville, was born there in 1809.
He afterwards moved to Salem and Westchester
but returned to Millington, and bought what is now
the town farm of William Cone, Esq., in 1828.
After living there just twenty years, he sold the
farm to the town, and moved to the Swan farm adjoining, where he died in 1851. His wife was
Anna Otis, of Salem. She survived him but a few
years. Their children were: Selden, Rachel Ann,
Lydia, Harriet, Nathaniel and Elizabeth. Selden
married Mercy Baker, of Montville. They died
childless. Rachel Ann married Col. Aaron T.
Niles. They had three sons and two daughters.
Hosford B. is the only living representative of the
family. Harriet died at the age of twenty. Lydia
married James Ely Swan. They had one son and
four daughters. James, the son, married Julia
Doane and moved to Colorado in 1871, where he is
now a successful farmer. His wife is dead. He is
the only living representative of the family. Of
the daughters, Pernella married David Emmons;
Harriet married Joseph H. Arnold; Catharine
married Sherwood Cone ; Caroline married Frank
W. Swan. All of them died in the early prime of
life of consumption. Dr. Nathaniel, now living at
the Landing, has long been well known as the lead
ing physician of the town. He married Juliet Mason, of New London. She died in 1874, leaving
ten children. Elizabeth Harris married Ephraim
Martin, and lives on the Dyer Emmons place in

Millington. They had two children : Harriet died
young. Anna married Charles Clark and lives in
Millington, on the William Ayres farm.

MARTIN.

Jonathan Martin, a weaver, came over from England and settled near Lyman Newbury. The old
cellar is now filled up. He had nine sons—Jonathan, William, Ephraim, Elihu, Peter, Samuel,
David, Joseph and ———

Jonathan 2d's children were Jonathan, Elihu,
Joseph, Esther, Mable, Oliver, Richard, Henry and
Wells.

William's were Hannah, Robert, William, Justin,
George, David, Lucy, Charles, Warren, Nancy and
Edwin.

Peter's were Julianna, Palmer, Maria, Janette
Almira, Henry, Edward, Ripley and Abby.

David's were Emma, Cone, George, Harriet and
Isaac.

Joseph's were Margaret, Niles, Ephraim, Esther,
Edgar, Isabella and Datus.

Samuel's were Mary, Samuel, Harlow, Henrietta,
Adaline, Hezekiah, Ellen and Catharine.

CHAPTER XV.

Goodspeed—Boardman.

Nathan Goodspeed moved to East Haddam from Barnstable, Cape Cod, Mass., between 1775-80, bought the lot on which the Gelston House stands and built a commodious two-story house thereon. He raised three children, viz.: Nathan, Joseph, and Anna. Nathan married and occupied the homestead. He left one daughter, Jerusha, who married Oliver Allen, of Norwich, and is now living in San Francisco or its vicinity. They have one son. Anna married Samuel Gilbert, of Hebron. Died about 1860, leaving one son, Nathan Gilbert, who resides in Norwich. Joseph married Laura Tyler, of Haddam, about 1812, and raised six children—George E., William H., Joseph F., Nathan T., Mary Anne, and Sophia. The only survivor of this family is William H., who is still an active business man of about sixty-three years, occupying the residence of his late father, who died at the age of sixty. His mother died at the age of forty-two, his brother George at fifty, his sister Mary Anne at forty, Sophia at twenty-four, Joseph and Nathan both at twenty-six.

Joseph Goodspeed was a clerk for the Rev. Solomon Blakeley, in a store in front of the lot now occupied by the Gelston House. After his marriage he carried on a store for several years in Haddam, hiring for that purpose a room in Timothy Shailor's house. He finally built a good-sized building which he used for a dwelling and store. Soon after this, Mr. Blakeley, wishing to give up his interest in mercantile business and being desirous of bringing his late favorite clerk back to East Haddam, persuaded him to buy out his stock of goods and lease the store. Mr. G. at once accepted the proposition of his friend, and moved back into the old store about 1814. He soon did a very thrifty business, and became a formidable rival of the staid old merchants of the Upper Landing. One of them so chafed over the growing popularity of the new store that he called upon its proprietor and notified him, through his position of first Selectman, that the store was on the highway and must be moved. Mr. G. replied that he knew one corner extended on the old highway about two feet, but was still five or six feet from any part of the road that was used—that the building had stood there over fifty years without complaint from any one, and that he would not attempt to move the building, but would move out of it as soon as he could make other arrangements. He was then ordered to move the building within twenty days, or the town would move it for him. When his good neighbor left, Mr. G. saddled his horse, and in two hours had contracted with Darius Dickinson aud the Messrs Bailey in Haddam for the erection of the store recently moved from the site now occupied by the new store, and in just forty-two days it was opened with the largest stock of new goods which had ever been introduced into the town.

Thus commenced a feud between the two villages which was kept up to a certain extent for many years. Indeed, even now there is an absence of that loving kindness, neighborly generosity, and mutual affection which Christian teachers enjoin and of which poets sing.

Mr. Goodspeed was a hard-working merchant, up early and late, and managed to draw not only from the best trade in town, but also sold goods to people of the adjoining towns. In fact, the new store of 1816 attracted as much attention as the magnificent new one of 1876, or sixty years later. George E. Goodspeed died in 1863. His widow, whose maiden name was Nancy G. Hayden, still resides at Goodspeed's Landing. Their son, Joseph H. is in a good position in Boston. Georgiana lives with her mother, and George E. is at school in New Haven. William H. Goodspeed married, in Baltimore, Miss Louise M. Robbins, formerly of Rocky Hill. She died young, leaving two children, William R., the present proprietor of the new store, and Louise R., who resides with her father in the family house, built by her grandfather Goodspeed in 1838. This house stands upon the site of the old Col. Chapman house, that the Chapman family occupied for many years, and afterwards by Rev. Mr. Blakeley, the son-in-law of Col. Chapman. It was occupied next and last by Jos. Goodspeed, who, after living in it twenty years, moved it across the street and attached it to

the then called Belden's Hotel. Subsequently, when
the Gelston House was built, the old Chapman
House was sold to Gideon Higgens, who took it
down, and out of a part of it built the house where
he resided at the time of his death in 1878. After
Col. Chapman's death, the most of the large farm
he owned came into the hands of his sons-in-law,
Rev. Stephen Blakeley and Capt. Oliver Attwood.
In 1831, Mr. Jos. Goodspeed bought that part of
the farm owned by Mr. Blakeley, and since their
father's death, George and William have bought of
the heirs of Oliver Attwood nearly all the farming
land left by him, and to-day the old Chapman farm
of 200 acres is in better condition than ever before.
The owner, Wm. H., seems to enjoy farming, though
one would naturally think he had enough to do without it. He claims that he likes to employ all the
men he can keep at work, and was never happier than
when he had 138 men at work on the following vessels in his yard in 1863: The steamers "Charles
Binton," "El Cid," "Sunshine," "Silver Star,"
"Sentinel," "Gen. Lyon," and schooners "Meteor"
and "Early Bird." This work, with the building of
the engines, etc., employing about 250 men in New
London, Mystic, and New York, kept him so busy
for a year or more that his average time for sleep
was only four or five hours out of the twenty-four
Even now he remains in his office till 9 P. M., reads
one or two hours, and is invariably in his office before five o'clock in the morning. He is also Vice-
President and General Manager of the H. & N. Y.

S. Boat Co., a corporation with a capital of $400,000, owning five steamers and a large property in real estate. Mr. Goodspeed has two children, Wm. R. and Louisa. Wm. R. has built one of the finest stores in the county, at Goodspeed's Landing, and carries on an extensive business in general merchandise.

NOTE :—The main points of the above sketch were furnished the writer by Wm. H. Goodspeed in 1875. He died Jan. 1st, 1882. His daughter Louisa died Oct. 21st, 1880.

BOARDMAN.

Thomas Curtis Boardman, born at Wethersfield, Conn., March 29th, 1798, came to Millington in 1815, as clerk for Noah Bulkley, in a store standing on the north side of the Green. He and Aaron T. Niles ran the same store for a while in partnership.

He moved to East Haddam Landing in 1836, and lived in the old "Tinker House," was elected cashier of the East Haddam Bank, the same year, and held the position till his sudden death September 18th, 1865. He was on the steamboat dock at East Haddam, when the Hartford steamer landed. The wooden cleat through which the cable ran, split as the boat strained upon it in the high wind, and the piece struck him on the head and breast. He fell dead at the feet of the writer.

Mr. Boardman married Sophronia, daughter of Hon. Wm. Palmer, by whom he had five children, four of them born in Millington.

Julia S., now living unmarried.

William B., married Georgiana R. S. Turner, of Boston. Have one daughter, Georgiana Chickering, named after the founder of the celebrated piano firm. They live in New York City.

Dorothea Amelia, died in 1842.

Francis married Mary Douglas. Children: Addie Minnie ; Jeanie Douglas ; Charles William.

Isabella Palmer ; drowned in Connecticut River in 1866.

Ellen Douglas.

Clarissa S. died in infancy.

Addie married Luther B. Williams of Rocky Hill. They have four children: Charles W. married Carrie Welch, of New Haven ; Jeanie married Wilbur S. Comstock.

Dorothea Amelia, 2d youngest daughter of Thos. Boardman, married Wilson C. Reynolds, of Lyme. He was post-master at East Haddam for 19 years. They have a fine residence at East Haddam, between the two Landings. Have three children : Gertrude Palmer ; Elsie Boardman ; Harry Wilson. Mrs. T. C. Boardman died in 1866.

CHAPTER XVI.

GREEN FAMILY.

James Green was born at Barnstable, Mass., September 17th, 1728. His father was William Green, of the same place, who died January 28th, 1756, aged over 70. His mother was Desire, daughter of John Bacon, Esq., also of Barnstable. His parents were married March 25th, 1709, and had seven children. Warren, the eldest, afterward removed to Middletown, Conn. The second, fourth and fifth were Desire, Sarah and Mary. The third child, William, also removed to Middletown. John, the sixth child, removed from Barnstable, but the records do not say whither. Some authorities say that James, the subject of this sketch, was engaged in the old French war; if so, he was quite young, for he was but seventeen years old at the time of the expedition against Louisburg. James Green removed to East Haddam, where he married, February 13th, 1754, Ruth, daughter of John and Elizabeth (Winslow) Marshall. Mrs. James Green was born at Freetown, Mass., April 1st, 1737, and lived in a house on the river bank, just north of one now occupied by Mr. Matthew Hubbard. I find among the East Haddam law records the fol-

lowing, which shows a determination to settle and
identify himself with the place as a landed proprietor :

1758, Aug. 4. Deed of land. Noah Smith, Jr.,
of Norwich, to James Green, of East Haddam.
Book vi.

1759, Nov. 29. 33 of Geo. II. Deed of land of
Nathaniel Tyler, to James Green·

1765, Apr. 24, Richard Alsop to James Green.
Consideration £60.

1765, Oct. so. Jabez Chapman to James Green.
Consideration £60. Deed of property southwest
of Green's lot.

1770, Jan. 20. Silvanus Tinker to James Green.
Consideration £60. Deed of land. wharf, and half
the store house house erected thereon.

1773 (13 Geo. III.). Ely Warner of Hartford to
James Green. £30.

1774 (14 Geo. III.). Richard Christopher to
James Green.

1777, May 32. Humphrey Lyon to James
Green.

1778, Nov. 10. Jehial and Rhoda Sexton, of
Waterbury, to Mr. J. Green.

1779, Mar. 16. Seth Willey to James Green.
£76 10s. Deed of land in Hadlyme.

1783, Oct. 4. Josiah Griswold, Middletown, to
Capt. James Green.

1784, Nov. 15. Caleb Gates to Capt. James
Green.

1786, May 4. Zachariah Chapman to Capt.
James Green.

Thirteen purchases of realty in that day and
place, and all within twenty-elght years, is unusual,
and there was bnt one sale, which was to Epaphroditus Champion, for £20, 6s. 8d., September 4th,
1786. He was not thirty years old when he pur-
chnsed his first real estate in East Haddam, and he
died possessed of all except the piece sold to Gen.
Champion. There is no record of the regiment to
which he was attached, except that it was a cavalry,
and he was with it as captain in some engagements
during the war, probably in the year 1776.

In a former chapter is described the different
residences of his sons and daughters at East Haddam Landing. Capt, Green was a leading citizen
of the town. There were annual elections then,
and we find Capt. James Green was chosen
"Brander of Horses" December 5th, 1766, and
every year to 1773. Every year from this until
1789 he held important offices in the town. Allusion has been made, in a former chapter, to a forge
near the spot where the Old Bank now stands. It
was there he made guns during the war, which
echoed the notes of the Declaration of Indepen-
dence on many a battle field to the satisfaction of
his present rebel associates, if not of his late royal
master, and East Haddam was all rebel. As early
as June 30th, 1774 it voted unanimous for a Declaration, and June 6th, 1778, adopted unanimously

the Articles of Confederation. They were prompt, generous and patriotic in furnishing arms, money and men.

Mrs. Ruth Green was baptised and they both entered the communion March 7th, 1773, at the meeting house of the First Society. Capt. Green died March 11th, 1809, and his widow November 27th, 1816. They were both buried in the Landing Cemetery. The old stones, which were falling to decay, were replaced with a marble slab by the sons of Capt. Green, with inscriptions as follows

SACRED

TO THE MEMORY OF

CAPTAIN JAMES GREEN,

WHO DIED MARCH 11, 1800

Æ 80.

ALSO OF

MRS. RUTH,

WIFE OF CAPTAIN JAMES GREEN,

WHO DIED NOV. 27, 1816

Æ. 79

They had eleven children, all born at East Haddam, to wit ;

Hannah Green, born March 14th, 1755.

Ruth, born May 2d, 1756 ; died January 21st, 1791.

James, born April 8th, 1758.

William Aug., born August 26th, 1760.

Benjamin, born August 31st, 1762.

Richard, born March 10th, 1765.

Ann (Nancy), born February 13th, 1768.

Timothy, born August 13th, 1771 ; died March March 19th, 1775.

Oliver, born August 16th, 1773.

Timothy 2d, born July 3, 1776.

Wilson, born July 10th, 1780.

CHAPTER XVII.

GIDEON HIGGINS.

Gideon Higgins, for over sixty-eight years a highly respected resident of East Haddam, died in that town on the first day of August, 1878, in the ninety-sixth year of his age. His prominency in all the civil affairs of the town, during so lengthy a period of time, entitles him to more than a passing notice in these pages. He was born in the town of Haddam, Conn., in that portion known as " Turkey Hill," on the 8th day of September, 1782. His parents, Hawes and Lucinda (Bushnell) Higgins, were of good repute in the community in which they lived. He was, from early youth, deeply impressed with the advantages of a good education, and, although in his boyhood, he saw but few opportunities to gratify his desire for information, yet those few he zealously improved. About three months at school each year was spared to him from his labor at farming, and at his father's trade of house and ship-building, until he arrived at the age of eighteen years, when he, for a brief time, attended school in Chester, under the instruction of the Rev. Mr. Mills. He lived in the town of his nativity until the age of twenty-two, when he went to the city of New York. This was about the year 1804, when that city numbered only 75,000 inhabitants. He remained there about two years engaged in ship building. At the expiration of that time he returned to Haddam, and in 1808 was made an Elector of the State of Connecticut in that town. He was married June 3d, 1809, to Ann Wright, daughter of William Wright, of Chatham, Conn., with whom he lived in the happiest relations until the time of her death, August 2d, 1852. They had five children, William W., Lucinda A., wife of Nathan Tyler, Catharine, Eliza M., wife of James M. Welch, and Mary S. Of these only one is now living—Catharine—who still lives in the old homestead at East Haddam. Mr. Higgins removed with his wife to East Haddam, November 10th, 1810, and commenced housekeeping in the house where the late Richard S. Pratt resided at the time of his decease. He became, during his residence in his native town, a member of the State Militia, and finally, in 1810, was chosen Captain of the Haddam Town Company, which position he held for the three succeeding years. When, during the war of 1812, the British troops made an attack upon and burnt our vessels at Essex, he, with nine others from this town volunteered, armed themselves, and took a row-boat for the scene of destruction, and, for a short time, took part in the attack upon the invaders, but soon after their arrival darkness ensued and enabled the Englishmen to make their escape with two men killed—one of whom was a lieutenant in rank.

In 1813, he removed his family to "Chapman's Landing," or "the Ferry," by both of which names it was then called — now universally known as "Goodspeed's Landing" — into the house then called the "Dr. Percival House." It stood on the site of the house where Whitby M. Smith now lives. Here he pursued his trade of "master ship builder" for many years, having a large force of men in his employ. In the year 1815 he purchased the land on which he erected the house which was his place of residence up to the time of his death. It was an unpromising piece of ground, but persevering industry made it a comfortable and pleasant home for over sixty-three years.

He, at various times filled responsible positions of public trust. He was a Deputy Sheriff of Middlesex County from October 3d, 1818, to June 1st, 1823. By the General Assembly of the State, in whom was vested the appointing power at the time, he was made the Sheriff of the county in 1827, which office he occupied for three years. In the years 1826 and 1827 he was elected to the lower House of the General Assembly, and subsequently also represented East Haddam during three other sessions of that body. From 1838 to 1842 he was a Commissioner of the County Court, and in 1834, one of the Judges of that Court. He was Judge of Probate for the District of East Haddam during the years 1844 and 1845.

Numerous minor offices of responsibility and

public trust in the gift of his fellow townsmen did Judge Higgins fill during his useful existence, covering nearly a century. It is sufficient to say that he performed the duties connected with them all creditably to himself and to the entire satisfaction of the public. He was sought for important private trusts and discharged them with perfect fidelity. His ad vice upon business matters and on law questions was considered valuable and his judgment was universally approved.

Politically, he was with the Whig party, and was a member of the Republican party from its organization.

He was always persistent and positive in the support of his political convictions, and never, except on very isolated occasions, when he was unavoidably prevented, did he omit to express his political faith at the ballot box in Electors' and Town Meeting. In fact his devotion to this duty of every citizen was very noteworthy. Being a radical anti-slavery man, he took great satisfaction in all proper measures looking to the emancipation of the slave, and was ever prepared to extend such assistance as lay in his power in the prosecution of that object. He was a man of courage—moral, intellectual and physical— and uncompromising in his convictions of duty. He never waited to learn the opinions of others in order to modify the expression of his own and shape them to some private advantage, but spoke as he thought, with a high sense of right, which always guided his sensibilities.

He was a practical temperance man, in every respect, at no time indulging in any of the physical excesses which impair or destroy health. With an active, energetic temperament, he possessed remarkable powers of physical strength and endurance. His arrival at the ripe old age of ninety-six years, in the possession of his mental faculties, and with an extraordinary amount of physical vigor for that age, was evidence of a healthy constitution, wisely preserved. At the age of ninety-five he shot a mischievous squirrel upon the top of one of his pear trees, and one week previous to his death, which resulted from an attack of dysentery, he was cutting the grass in his orchard with the briskness of a much younger man.

His private character was without a stain. His integrity was unquestioned. To his excellence as a citizen he added a true Christian character, which he manifested in profession and practice.

Although favoring the Second Adventist doctrine, he was free from the taint of sectarian bigotry, and cordially welcomed all manifestations of a Christian life.

His old Bible, so long and faithfully used, bears upon each page evidences of how diligently it was perused, and how well it was loved, and with its teachings in his heart, he closed his earthly career with great hope and assurance of eternal life.

CHAPTER XVIII.

BRAINARD—GATES—GELSTON.

Among the early settlers from Haddam was Daniel Brainard, Jr., who settled at the lower end of the Creek Row, near the spring just below the Royal Ayres place. His father, Daniel, came from England when eight years of age, and was the ancestor of the Brainards in this country. He settled in Haddam in 1662, and was a prosperous and influential man, a justice of the peace in the town, and a deacon in the church. The family is very numerous in this part of the country, and has always ranked among the highest in wealth and influence. Two doctors, Daniel and Hezekiah, were eminent physicians; Thomas, Israel, Timothy G., Elijah and Nehemiah were popular ministers of the gospel; Hon. Jeremiah and Hon. Hezekiah gained much distinction as legislators and judges; while David and Rev. John earned world-wide renown as missionaries among the Indians. The two latter were children of the Hon. Hezekiah. Their older sister married Gen. Joseph Spencer, of Millington, in whose family David, the eminent missionary, lived for four years. David's labors were for a long time with the Lenni-Lenape and other tribes along the

Delaware River. The finest church in Easton, Pa., is Brainard Church, a fitting monument to his name and fame.

Daniel Brainard, the original settler. had eight children, as follows : Daniel, Jr., Hannah, James, Joshua, William, Caleb, Elijah and Hezekiah. All the Brainards in this country are said to be descendents of these children. Of our townsmen, William O. and Abby Brainard, Mrs. Silas Nichols, Judah and Benjamin Lewis, Milton, John, and Frank Brainard, and many of the Days in Westchester, are descendents of Daniel, Jr. The Gates' descended from Hannah. Joshua Brainard's residence is marked by the old cellar mound just south of Selden Brainard's, and from this branch descended Col. Orren Warner, Brainard Emmons, Miss Lucretia Brainard and Mrs. Blakeman. Joshua was commander of the first military company formed in East Haddam. Erastus and Silas, the Portland quarry owners, are descendants of James. Selden T. Brainard, David B. and George Sexton, of East Haddam. Fisk and Henry Brainard, of Haddam Neck, and Cornelius Brainard, of Higganum, are descendants of William. Caleb was the ancestor of David Brainard, of East Haddam. Mrs. Francis Palmer is a descendant of Elijah. John G. C. Brainard, a brilliant writer, Editor of the *Hartford Mirror* and author of a book of poems, from which the poem " Matchit Moodus," in Chapter V. was copied, was also a native of

this town.   The estate of Daniel Lord, deceased,
is a part of the farm formerly owned by George
Gates, and later by Phineas.   The old house stands
a little north of the present dwelling.   The house
owned by Aristarchus and Seth Daniels, was built
by Joseph Gates in 1774: its peaked roof still at-
tracts attention, and in its youth, it must have been
considered quite a stately edifice.   It was first de-
signed for a court house, and afterwards made over
into a tavern.   It was purchased in 1804 by the
Daniels, who came from Haddam Neck.   Joseph
Gates, its builder, was the son of Joseph Gates,
born in 1722.   In regular descent by this line come
Orren and Epaphroditus, also Uri, the brother of
Orren.   The latter Joseph was also the father of
Bazaleel Gates, who was the father of Brainard,
Hannah, and Beriah.   All of the above, of the last
generation, have died within the last ten years.
The homestead of the elder Joseph stood a little
north of the large house where Uri lived and died,
and which was built by his father.   The house purchased of Brainard and Hannah by George I. Kipp,
was built by Bazaleel in 1800.   The old road on
which it stands, now closed for many years, was
once a main thoroughfare from Moodus to Bashan.

Deacon Maltby Gelston, a farmer in Bridgehamp-
ton, L. I., during the Revolution, fled with his
family as refugees from British rule to East Haddam.   He occupied a house standing on the bank

of the Connecticut River, near the one recently built by David Watrous. A part of the old foundation can still be traced. After the war closed he returned to his farm on Long Island. William Gelston, his seventh child, on his return from the war in the year 1781, married Asenath Sayres, daugher of Matthew Sayres, who was then one of the largest land owners in the town of East Haddam. He erected the large house near the Episcopal Church, in the year 1760. William Gelston, soon after his marriage, purchased the property on which the Gelston House now stands, where he lived until 1826. A part of the old mansion is now attached to the present house.

Through purchase, and inheritance by his wife, he became possessed of a large tract of land, and for convenience he concluded to move. He bought of Samuel Crowel, the house now occupied by the Gelston family. Soon after moving here in 1826 he sold his place at the Ferry to Joseph Goodspeed.

More than twenty years ago the Gelston House Company was formed, the largest stockholders of the Company being Hugh Gelston, of Baltimore, and George S. Gelston, of Fort Hamilton, two sons of William Gelston. The present hotel was built and named the Gelston House. Mr. Gelston reared a family of seven sons and three daughters. He was sheriff for twenty years and filled many town offices. He died at the age of eighty-five. His son William followed him as the possessor of the landed estate, and died in 1875, at the age of eighty-nine years. He left four children Maltby, John, Mrs. West, of NewLondon and Lucy.

CHAPTER XIX.

CONE.

Daniel Cone, born in 1626, came over from Edinboro, Scotland, and settled in Haddam with his four sons, in 1670. He left one son in Scotland. The family moved to East Haddam a few years afterwards, built a log hut, and settled on the farm recently purchased of Jonathan Cone, by Benjamin Edwards. Until this transfer, it has remained in the Cone family. Daniel died in 1706, and was buried in Haddam. His sons were Daniel, Jared, Stephen and Caleb. One of them retained the homestead ; one settled on the spot where Zachary Cone now lives ; one near Palmer Place, now owned by Mrs. Doane ; the other near Elijah Warner's. The homestead finally came into the possession of Capt. Stephen, who, in turn, bequeathed it by will to Stephen, John and Reuben. Capt. Stephen was buried in the Methodist cemetery, in 1752. He occupied a house standing a few rods east of the one above referred to. It was demolished a few years ago. He erected a new dwelling on a spot about ten rods north or the present house, the foundations of which are now completely obliterated. The house was two stories in front and one in rear. The settlers in those early days used to assemble at times and surround the wolves, starting as far as Middle Haddam, and driving them down on the Neck, where they became good targets for the hunters.

Stephen used to interest his grandchildren by relating how the family often sat on the back door-step and listened to the howling of the wolves as they were driven through the forest. At that time the highway used to run from Fuller's Landing, near Scofield's, in an easterly direction, and struck the Moodus road, near Oliver Emmons'. The house where Edwards now lives stands directly in this old highway. The property next descended to Stephen and Thomas Cone. Thomas occupied the land where Chloe Cone now lives. She was a direct descendant, her father being Joshua, who was the son of Joel, who was the grandson of Thomas. Stephen third retained the old place, which from him descended to Elisha, thence to Elisha second, thence to Stephen, thence to Jonathan. The Thomas branch is now represented by Chloe, and her nephew Theodore. Theodore served in the rebellion as Colonel in the Confederate army, and is now practicing law in Georgia. The daughters of Stephen and Thomas intermarried with the Gates, Fullers, Chapmans and Williams, thus creating a relationship which extends to nearly all the old families in town.

Zachary, Robert S., Wm. E., George, and the late Helen Cone, of Millington, are direct descendants of Jared by different branches. Zachary married

Elizabeth, daughter of the late Rev. Isaac Parsons, and retains the old place.   A. Jared, Jr., moved to Millington, married a daughter of the early Matthew Smith (see Smith family) and settled on the Bala- hack road, which runs west from Edwin Emmons. The old chimney stack still stands.   Then, the road now running by Ephraim Martin's did not exist. The old road was several rods west of the present one, but terminated near the same point.

Jared died in 1742, Nehemiah, his son, lived at the Christopher Marsh place, and died in 1819.   His children were Mary, Newel, Statira, Sarah, Jared, Lucy and Betsey.

George, the father of Helen R. and George, Jr. lived here.   Helen R., left Millington in 1838, and has been in the wholesale fruit business, near Ful- ton Ferry, New York, for about forty years. George, Jr., died in Georgia.

Deacon William E. Cone, is a son of Newel.   He has always resided in East Haddam, has often repre- sented the town in the State Senate and House of Representatives, has filled the most important town offices, and always performed his duties with great fidelity   His only son, William A., has recently built a new residence at Goodspeed's Landing, where he is engaged in the insurance business, representing some of the best companies in the country. William R. Cone, president of the Ætna Bank, Deacon James E. Cone, and the late Sylvanus F. Cone, of Hartford, were from East Haddam.

The following notices were cut from the Connecticut Valley *Advertiser*, in 1886.

OBITUARY.

SYLVANUS F. CONE.

Mr. Sylvanus F. Cone, brother of Deacon James E. Cone and William R. Cone, president of the Ætna Bank, died yesterday morning at 7 o'clock, of typhoid and malarial fever, at his residence on Warrenton street, Hartford. Mr. Cone was born in East Haddam, in August, 1814, and moved to this city in 1835, since which time he has resided here continually. He always took a warm interest in public affairs, rarely, or never failing to exercise his rights as a citizen. He was for many years a member of the board of selectmen as well as an assessor, and filled other important trusts, always performed his duties with scrupulous fidelity. He was possessed of a most genial and kindly disposition, retaining his youthful feelings and appearance to a wonderful degree, and was esteemed and beloved by a large circle of friends and acquaintances. He leaves a wife and four sons, Joseph H., William E., and John B. Cone of this city, and Augustus F. Cone, who resides in Cincinnati, and one daughter, Miss Ella B. Cone.

DEATH OF WILLIAM E. CONE.

Deacon William E. Cone, one of the aged residents of our village, and in days gone by, one of the prominent men of the town, died on Saturday evening last. He was born in Millington eighty years ago last September, and nearly all of his four score years had been passed in his native town. For many years he was the general manager for W. E. Nichols & Co., twine manufacturers of this village, and his business ability was recognized and his counsel sought by many. He represented the town of East Haddam in the Legislature of 1862 ; was re-elected in '63' and was a member of the Senate from

this senatoral district (then the nineteenth) in 1865 and '66·
He had also at various times held minor positions of trust
within the gift of his townsmen. His political opponents were
not political enemies, for his candor, under all circumstances,
won the respect of those who, perhaps, were at variance with
him. He was a faithful and willing worker in the cause of
temperance, and though not over demnostrative, his broad influence was ever for the right. He early in life united with
the church, and for thirty-seven years he had been one of the
deacons of the First Congregational Church of this town. He
was a man careful in his judgment ; a true Christian, and his
death was the closing of a well-spent life. The funeral service was held Thursday afternoon, at the Methodist Church,
and was conducted by Rev. S. McCall, assisted by Revs. S.
W. Robbins, of Manchester, G. W. Wright and J. B. Con-
nell. The large number present on the occasion, notwithstanding the severe rain storm prevailing at the time, bore evi
dence of the great respect in which the deceased was held in this
community. It is a fact worthy of mention, that during the
long life of Deacon Cone, probably no man in town had kindly
officiated as funeral director on so many occasions.

Of the early settlers, near Elijah Warner's, Isaac
Cone was a direct descendant and owned the farm
extending from Bald Hill to Miner Gillett's, and
lived where G. R. Tracy now lives. The mother of
Timothy Holmes and Mrs. Hubbard Ayres are also
direct descendants of this branch. The family name
of this branch in East Haddam seems to have be
come extinct with the death of Robert D. Cone, for
many years a school teacher. He was a bachelor
and lived for several years with Jonathan Clark.

The old gambrel-roofed house, standing on the old
road, running west from Daniel Peck's, was Erastus

Cone's. He was the uncle of Lord Wellington. Erastus' father was Israel, who was the son of Israel. The father of William H. and Charles, was Samuel Cone, who lived where Wm. C. Gates now lives. Just east of Gates, is an old chimney, which marks the house where lived Samuel's father, Deacon Nathaniel. One of his sons went to East Hampton, and from him the present Cones in Chatham descended. Nathaniel was elected deacon of Millington church, about one year before his death, which occurred April 15, 1790. He had eight sons in the Revolutionary war. Helon Cone settled in Foxtown, among whose rocks he delved out quite a fortune. He left by will ten thousand dollars in trust, to be loaned at low rates of interest to deserving young men of the town, the principal and accumulated interest to be so used forever. Time would render the possibilities of such a fund beyond computation, and he was advised that such a provision would hardly stand the test of law. He revised it and demised that when the sum shall reach seventy-five thousand dollars it shall be applied to the building of a free academy in Millington Society. He died in 1878. His nephew, William H., son of Samuel, died three years before. He was the largest land owner in the town, and for many years exerted a great influence in town affairs. He left one son, Willian Lyman, now living on Millington Green. Thus it may be seen that Israel and Samuel formed different branches of the original family, but all of the name of Cone in the United States, forming numerous and wide-spreading branches, may trace their origin to that same old trunk which is represented by our Daniel Cone, who settled in Haddam in 1670.

CHAPTER XX.

HALL AND SMITH.

The old house where Jedediah Hall died, a few
years since, has remained in the Hall family since
the early settlement, until its recent sale. Here
Dyer's father, Samuel Hall, carried on his trade of
scythe-making in a shop near Oliver Clark's. He
was a man of considerable influence. His wife was
a spry little woman, with complexion quite dark. In
her day slavery was not extinct even in Connecticut,
and it is related of her that a stranger, who came to
see Mr. Hall, mistook her position and accosted her
with the question : " Where is your master ?" " I
wish you to understand, sir," she replied, " that I
have no master but God." Thomas Hall lived a
short distance east of the Dyer Hall house, at the
corner of the Town Hill road, near Bashan Pond.
The old chimney stack still remains. The old road
leading from Oliver Palmes' to the Halsey Brown
place is an ancient land-mark. Here, at the north
end of the road, lived many of the Spencers, and
near the south end lived several families of Smiths,
the ancestor of them all being Matthew, who
came from Lyme to East Haddam on the 6th day
of November, A. D. 1706, at the age of 22. He

located on the spot where Alden now lives. Soon
after coming here he married Sarah Mack, and built
a house a short distance east of the present house.
There he, and afterwards his son Matthew, lived till
the year 1778, when the present house was built by
Matthew Smith second.

From him it was bequeathed by will to Jeremiah,
his third son. From him Jeremiah, Jr., purchased
it in 1802, and from thence it came to the present
heirs, being the fifth generation in direct descent,
and making one hundred and seventy years that the
place has remained in the family. The present
house stands to-day as it was built over a hundred
years ago. A tall and stately mansion, it overlooks
all the dwellings of the plain. Then, in the scarcely
broken wilderness, it must have been regarded as
some lordly manor, the center of the rude civilization of the place and times, as it was the birth
place of a numerous and influential family. Matthew Smith and Sarah Mack had eight children, as
follows :

Mary, married Joseph Cone.
Ruth, married Jared Cone.
Lydia, married Josiah Arnold.
Sarah, married Thomas Rogers.
Susanna, married Nehemiah Tracy.
Elizabeth, died unmarried.
Thomas, married Hannah Gates, Feb. 9th, 1737.
Matthew 2d, married Sarah Church, January
16th, 1745.

Matthew Smith, 1st, died December 6th, 1751, aged 67, and was buried at the Cone burying ground. Sarah, his wife, died January 18th, 1755, aged 71, and was buried by his side.

Matthew 2d, born A. D. 1722, and Sarah Church had seven children, five sons and two daughters, as follows :

Asa was born 1747. He died when about 21 He was found dead near the residence of the late William H. Aynes, where he went to attend a social gathering in the evening. He was not found until after a search of two days, and then but a short distance from the house. The cause of his death is to this day wrapped in mystery.

Elizabeth, born November 12th, 1750 ; married Oliver Ackley.

Matthew 3d, born May 12th, 1753 ; married Aseneth Anable in December, 1777.

Azariah was born in 1755. He died in 1778, and was buried in the Smith burial ground.

Jeremiah was born March 29th, 1758, and was married to Temperance Comstock June 17th, 1784, and by will became possessor of the old homestead.

Calvin was born in 1760 ; married Anna Anable January 15th, 1784. In company with Matthew, his brother, he moved to Middlefield, in Western Massachusetts, where they raised large families. Their descendants, yet living in that vicinity, are numerous and very respectable.

Sarah, was born in 1762 ; she married John Park and removed from the town.

Returning to Jeremiah, who married Temperance Comstock, we find that they had seven children—four sons and three daughters—as follows :

Jeremiah, Jr., was born November 21st, 1786, and married Ruthy Ackley April 27th, 1809.

Temperance was born October 27th, 1788 ; married Joseph Ackley, October 27th, 1805 ; died February 29th, 1812.

Sophia was born May 13th, 1793 ; she married Joseph Brainard.

Abner C. was born March 29th, 1796. He married Electa Warner, and now resides a few rods south of the old homestead.

Erastus was born April 19th, 1799. He married Ann Allen, and resides with his son William on Mt. Parnassus.

Julia J. was born July 8th, 1801. She married C. C. Gates, and is now living in Moodus. There are two branches of the Smith family in this vicinity, both of which, however, descended from the first Matthew. The divergence commenced with Thomas, his son, who built a house nearly in front of the Halsey Brown house, on the corner of the road leading to Aristarchus Daniels. The remains of the old cellar are yet visible. He had three sons—Matthew, Thomas and Samuel. Matthew subsequently built the house a little north of the old homestead, where Fluvia now lives, by which family it was inherited. Matthew 2d, of this branch, had twelve children, six sons and six daughters. The latter married as follows

Hannah married Stephen Fuller.
Lydia married Jabez Fuller.
Thankful married Irad Fuller.
Esther married Josiah Gates.
Olive married Jonas Sparks.
Dorothy married William Palmer.

Matthew lived and died on the old place. Asa located in Moodus, where Emory Lewis now lives and was the father of Watrous B. and Asa, Jr. Jonah moved West, where he died. The other sons died when children. Of our townsmen, Alden and Edmund, it will be observed that the former is a descendant of the first branch, the latter of the second, or Thomas, branch. Most of Alden's relations moved to Massachusetts ; Edmunds to Missouri.

CHAPTER XXI.

SPENCER FAMILY.

Sergeant Jared Spencer, of "The New Town," Cambridge, Mass., then of Lynn, and afterwards one of the first settlers of Haddam, Conn., made Ensign Sept. 1675, by the Council of Hartford, had eleven children.

SECOND GENERATION.

2. Samuel Spencer, (sixth child of Jared Spencer), of Millington. M. 1st. Hannah, widow of Peter Blachford, (or Blachfield), also widow Thomas Hungerford, New London, and daughter Isaac Wiley, of New London, 1673. M. 2d. Marriam, widow of John Wiley, of Haddam, and daughter of Miles Moore, New London, 1689. Mirriam Spencer survived her husband, who died August 7, 1705, leaving four children.

THIRD GENERATION

3. Deacon Isaac Spencer (son of Samuel), baptized Dec. 24, 1704, married Mary Selden, October 2, 1707. She was born 5 Mar., 1689; her parents were Rebecca (Church) Selden, from Hadley, Mass. Isaac Spencer was chosen deacon of 1st Ch., E. H., June 26, 1734, and died Feb. 10, 1751, aged 71 years; they had —— children, viz.

Mary, b July 24, 1710,

Rebecca, b Aug. 1, 1712,

Joseph, b Oct. 3, 1714, bapt. Jan. 1715.

Esther, b Dec. 16, 1716,

Jared, b Nov. 5, 1718, bap. Dec. 7, 1718,

Elihu, b Feb. 12, 1721, afterwards Rev. Elihu
Spencer, of the College of N. Y., and father of
Mrs. Jonathan Dickinson Sargeant, whose son,
Jno. Sergeant, b 1780, was candidate for Vice Pres.
U. S., 1832.

Isaac, b May 3, 1723,

Mehitable, b May 29, 1725,

Hannah, bap. Nov. 26, 1727,

Anna, b Nov. 29, 1729,

Israel, b Jan. 30, 1731–32, m Eliza Marsh, Oct.
18, 1753.

FOURTH GENERATION.

Hon. Joseph Spencer, (eldest son of Isaac), married Aug. 2, 1738, Martha, dau. Hon. Hezekiah and
Dorothy (Hobart) Brainard. Joseph Spencer was
admitted to church at Millington, March 23, 1746.
He was Assistant (Senator) Conn., 1774 and 1775 ;
Judge of Probate 1775. " June 30, 1774, in town
meeting duly warned—Hon. Joseph Spencer
chosen moderator, a unanimous vote was recorded
for a Declaration of American Rights." " Jan. 6,
1778, Articles of Confederation were unanimously
adopted." He presided on this occasion also, and
frequently besides. (E. H. Records.) In May,
1778, he was made a member of the Council of

Safety. In the Colonial army 1756, he was a Major, and afterwards Colonel, and must have served with some distinction, for at the commencement of the war with Great Britain, the State of Connecticut turned immediately to him as a leader, and the Assembly, in the month of March, 1775, appointed " Col. David Wooster a Major General, and Col. Joseph Spencer, and Israel Putnam to be Brigadier Generals," thus making him second in rank in the State.

The war had now actually begun, and Washington had been chosen Commander-in-Chief. Congress proceeded to appoint four Major-Generals and eight Brigadier-Generals : they named Ward C. Lee, Schuyler and Putnam for the former positions, and Pomeroy, Montgomery, Wooster, Heath, Joseph Spencer, Thomas, Sullivan and Greene for the latter, thus making Spencer's rank tenth in the Colonial army ; but there is nothing which touches a soldier quicker than to see his subordinates placed above him, and there is nothing so destructive to discipline as such promotions, except for cause. Many felt this besides Spencer, who was at first so offended that he left camp, but was soon induced to return. Gen. Seth Pomeroy, the senior Briga dier, refused to serve, and Spencer took rank next to Putnam in the army at Boston. In the division of the army by Washington into three grand divisions, the command of the right wing, on Roxbury Heights, was given to Gen. Ward, the senior Major

General, and with him were associated Spencer and Thomas, the ranking Brigadiers.

In August 1776, Spencer was commissioned a Major-General by Congress.

I have never seen a portrait or likeness of any kind of Gen. Spencer, and this is the more strange from the fact that John Trumbull, son of the patriot Gov. Trumbull, of Conn., first went into the army with Spencer, and it was during the time he was with him that he made those drawings of the enemies' works which won the favorable notice of Washington, and secured him the position of aide-de-camp on the staff of the Commander-in-Chief. Trumbull painted most of the military and public men of that day, but seems to have omitted Spencer.

Spencer's was the last brigade which left Boston for New York ; this was on the 4th of April, 1776.

During the occupation of New York, Spencer occupied a redoubt on the present Pike street, between Munroe and Cherry streets, called Spencer Redoubt. He also held the left at Harlem, of the line of defense extended across the city from the Hudson to the Harlem at McGowan's Pass. These various positions are now so covered up by the march of population and the growth of the city, that they are past recognition, except the pass at the northern extremity of Central Park.

On the 29th of August, 1776, Washington called a council of war on Long Island, at the Dutch

Stone Church, near the junction of the present Fulton and Flatbush avenues in the city of Brook lyn. The following officers were present, viz. · Washington, Putnam, Spencer, Mifflin, McDougal, Parsons, Scott, Wadsworth and Parsons, and on the 7th of September the question as to the expediency of retaining New York city came before the council. and the majority voted to retain it. On the 12th of September, however, it resolved on the evacuation, with only three dissenting votes, which were given by Heath, Joseph Spencer and James Clinton.

Maj. Gen. Spencer was soon after placed in command of all the American forces in the State of Rhode Island, and July 11, 1777, Maj. Gen. Pres cott, the English commander, fell into his hands as a prisoner of war. He was treated kindly by his captor, and in a short time was sent to Gen. Washington, who exchanged him for Gen. Chas. Lee, a prisoner since Dec. 1776.

Gen. Spencer arranged an expedition in·Sept., 1777, which was actually embarked, to cross to R. I., and surprise the enemy. At the last moment, having learned that the English commander was apprised of his plans, he countermanded the order. The facts proved that he had acted rightly, for the enemy had determined to allow them to land, and then by destroying their boats, to cut off their retreat and make them prisoners. Congress ordered an investigation into the affair, to ascertain why the expedition was not prosecuted, and Spencer in

indignation at the implied censure, resigned his com-
mission, and Gen. Sullivan was sent to R. I. to suc-
ceed him. On the 30th of August, 1778, Spencer
assisted in Sullivan's retreat, and this seems to have
been his last military service. He then returned
to his home on the banks of the Connecticut, and
doubtless intended to remain there ; but his native
State had not forgotten him, and he was elected to
represent it in Congress.

He married a second time in 1756, Hannah
Brown, of Waterbury, widow of Mr. Southmaid ;
she united with the church, Dec. 13, 1788.

I find in the E. H. town Records, "Col. Jos.
Spencer was elected deacon of the Millington
Society, Nov. 20, 1767 ;" afterward the record shows
that "he was excused from service during the Revolution," and again, " re-elected April 4, 1788."
The last town record reads, "Hon. Jos. Spencer,
died Jan. 13, 1789, aged 74,"—to be exact, 74 years,
3 mos., and 10 days. He had by his first marriage
three daughters and two sons, and by the second
marriage four sons and four daughters.

FIFTH GENERATION.

(5) Martha Spencer, (daughter Hon. Jos.) b May
8, 1739 ; died Feb. 24, 1739-40.

(5) Martha Spencer, (daughter Hon. Jos.) not
entered among the births recorded at Millington ;
married June 14, 1759, Joseph Cone, Jr., who was
born in E. H., Nov. 2, 1735 ; they had five child
ren : Conant Cone, b July 6, 1760, was father of

Spencer H. Cone, D. D., the eminent Baptist divine of N. Y. City, some years since. The second child, Alice, was born Feb. 18, 1762, and the others, Prudence, John and Martha, were baptized Sept. 8, 1868.

(5) Anne Spencer, (dau. Hon. Jos.) bapt. Millington, March 30, 1746.

(5) Joseph Spencer, (son Hon. Jos.) bapt. Millington, July 22, 1750 ; he married —— ——. I have a record of but one child (6) Elizabeth Spencer, who married Hon. Lewis Cass, Major-General U. S. A.., Governor of the State of Michigan, U. S. Senator, and Secretary of War in the Cabinet of President Jackson, 1831 to 1837.—He was Democratic Candidate for President against Zachary Taylor.

(5) Nehemiah Spencer, (son Hon. Jos.) bapt. Mill., Dec. 24, 1752.

(5) Millicent Spencer, (dau. Hon. Jos.) bapt. Mill., March 20, 1757 ; joined the church April 5, 1789 ; m. Dec, 18, 1813, Rev. Elijah Parsons, pastor of the First Society at E. Haddam.

(5) Hon. Isaac Spencer (son of Hon. Jos.) bapt. Dec. 9, 1759, married Lucretia, daughter of Harris Colt. Mr. Spencer was for many years Treasurer of the State of Connecticut.

Jared Spencer, Esq., (son Hon. Jos.) born June 5, 1762, a twin, bapt. Mill. July 25, 1762. At the age of twenty-two he graduated (A. B.) from Yale College in the class of 1784, after which he fitted himself for his profession as Counsellor at Law, which he practiced until his death. He married

Nov. 29, 1789, Ann Green (church records say Nov. 30.) She was the sixth child of Captain James and Ruth Marshall Green, born 13th Feb. 1768, bapt. Mar. 14, 1773, joined the church June 5, 1796, and died Nov. 11, 1855, aged 87 years and nine months. Esquire Spencer perished in a snow-storm Nov. 11, 1820, aged 58, leaving him surviving four children, one, an infant, having died in 1802.

(6) Nancy b. May 29, 1791, bapt. July 6, 1796, joined the church May 1, 1814, married Capt. Thomas Bruce, of Portland, Conn. left two children.

(6) Richard Green bapt. May 4, 1800, removed to Canada where he married Sophia Lake, of Vermont. He died of cholera 1834, leaving one son.

(6) Mary (Polly) b Sept. 12, 1793, bapt. July 3, 1796, died Sept. 7, 1860, aged 66.

(6) Lucretia b Sept. 12, 1793, bapt. July 3, 1796, died April 26, 1858, aged 63. These ages are from the tomb stones, and if the dates are correct the former lacked but 5 days of 67 years, and the latter was 64 years, 7 months and 14 days.

(5) Mary Spencer (dau. Hon. Jos.) born June 5 1762, bapt. July 25, 1762, a twin, married Turner Miner.

(5) Seth Spencer (son Hon. Jos.) bapt. Jan. 20, 1765.

(5) Hannah Spencer (dau. Hon. Jos.) bapt. Nov. 15, 1767, married Rev. Mr. Skinner.

(5) Betty Spencer (dau. Hon. Jos.) bapt. Mar. 18 1770, married Selden Warner.

(5) Nehemiah Spencer (son Hon. Jos) bapt. May 24, 1772, married Feb. 14, 1793, Betsy Swan.

(For the above genealogy of the Spencer family, I am indebted to Mr. Richard H. Green of Brooklyn)

CHAPTER. XXII

PROMINENT MEN.

The readers of the Old Chimney Stacks, have probably observed that East Haddam, and particularly Millington, has been the birth-place or residence of many prominent men, whose names have been illustrious in connection with our national and state governments; men who have adorned the higher and nobler professions of life; men, and women too, to whom we can refer with pride. Many of them sleep in our church yards, though dead, yet living; many went forth and have never returned from the fields where they so nobly toiled; some still live to adorn their chosen professions. I will now record some of the prominent names which occur to me, and regret that I am unable to make the list complete.

Hon. Joseph Spencer, whose history is here given, was a native of Millington, and lived and died at the Old Stack, just south of Lyman Cone's. His brother, Rev. Elihu Spencer, of the College of New Jersey, was born in Millington. His grandson, John Sargeant, was candidate for Vice President of the United States, in 1832.

Rev. Spencer H. Cone, the eminent Baptist Divine, was born in Millington, just south of E. F.

Peck's. For a number of years he stood at the head of the Baptist church in New York City.

Elizabeth Spencer, daughter of Joseph, Jr., of Millington, beeame the wife of the Hon. Lewis Cass, candidate for President in 1848.

Hon. Isaac Spencer, of Millington, was for many years Treasurer of the State of Connecticut.

David Brainard, the eminent Missionary among the Indians, was a brother of Hon. Joseph Spencer's wife, and resided several years in Millington, when a youth.

One of the most remarkable men of the age, was Dr. Eliphalet Nott, who lived during several years of his boyhood on the old road running north from the old Austin Beebe House in Millington. He lived here with relatives, having been left an orphan at quite an early age. During his early life he had to endure many of the hardships of poverty. For want of shoes he was forced to go barefooted most of the year. When quite young, he had an unquenchable thirst for knowledge, and, notwithstanding his limited opportunities, and the obstacles he had to encounter, at the age of nineteen he stood the examination for the degree of Master of Arts, and actually had the degree conferred upon him by Brown's University without his having attended college a single day. He chose the vocation of the ministry, and after the usual three years' study, was ordained at the age of twenty-two. He was married soon after, and with his bride, on horseback, started off on their wedding-trip to what was then the far West.   They stopped and made a settlement at the new village of Cherry Valley, about fifty miles west of Albany.   Soon after his settlement, the fame of his talents reaching Albany, he was invited to become the pastor of one of its principle churches, which invitation he accepted. While here, he preached that famous sermon upon the death of Hamilton, which attracted universal attention, and which still ranks as one of the most eloquent and striking ever delivered in the United States.   Seven years after he came to Albany, he was called to the presidency of Union College, in the building up and management of which he displayed talents for business that would have sufficed for the government of a nation.   He was also the inventor of the famous " Nott Stove " for burning coal, the patents of which procured a vast revenue, so that when he died, he was one of the richest men in the State of New York, west of Albany.

In the fiftieth year of his presidency, he gave to Union College as a permanent endowment, the sum of six hundred and ten thousand dollars.   He held his position for sixty-one years, and died in the ninety-third year of his age.

Born before the Revolution, inheriting an almost perfect bodily constitution, with talents of the highest order, which were used only for the benefit of mankind he lived to see the close of the Rebellion, bequeathing to the world a name and a fame that will never die.

CHAPTER XXIII.

Prominent Men Continued.

East Haddam boasts of the unusual honor of having two members of Congress at one time, both of whom were elected for several terms under the old law for electing Congressmen by general ticket. These were Gen. Epaphroditus Champion and Jonathan O. Mosley. Gen. Champion lived at the old Tyler Place in East Haddam Landing. He was a member of the General Assembly in 1793. He had command of the 24th Regiment of the Connecticut State Militia, before his election to Congress.

The following letter from General George Washington to General Champion, of this town, will be read with interest. At the date given, General Champion was commissary general of provisions for the army. The original letter is in the possession of Harvy J. Brooks, Haddam Neck:

CAMP VALLEY FORGE, FEB. 17th, 1778.

SIR : — The present situation of the army is the most melancholy that can be conceived. Our supplies of provisions of the flesh kind for some time past have been very defficient and irregular. A prospect now opens of absolute want, such as will make it impossible to keep the army much longer from disolution, unless the most vigorous and effectual measures are pursued to prevent it. Jersey, Pennsylvania and Maryland are now entirely exhausted. All the beef and pork already collected in them, or that can be collected, will not, by any means, support the army one month longer. Further to the southward some quantities of provisions have been procured ; but if they were all on the spot, they would afford but a very partial and temporary supply. The difficulty of transportation is great. The distance will not allow it to be effected by land carriage ; and the navigation up Chespeak Bay is interrupted by the enemy's vessels, which makes it very precarious when we shall get any material relief from that quarter. If every possible exertion is not made use of there, to send us immediate and ample supplies of cattle, the most fatal consequences most ensue. I have much confidence in your zeal and activity, and trust, upon this occasion, they will be exerted in a peculiar manner, to hurry on to camp all the cattle you may be able to purchase.

I am, sir, your most obedient servant,

GEO. WASHINGTON.

Henry Champion, Esq.

EPAPHRODITUS CHAMPION'S LIST, FOR 1813 :

1 head $60, 2 cows $14, 2 horses, $10, $20..........	$94.00
50 acres mowing and clear pasture, a $1.34...........	67.00
37 " brush pasture and wood land, a .34.......... ..	12.58
1 Phaeton $100, one chaise say $30.................	130.00
1 silver watch $10, one clock $20..................	30.00
1 house 11 fire places, a $5.....................	55.00
2 one-story stores, $10............................	20.00
30 oz. plate a $1.11 a 6 pet...................... ...	5.33
3,700 dollars bank stock a 3 pet	111.00

$524.91

Col. Mosley lived but little over a mile north of Gen. Champion, on the place now owned by Wm. J. Morgan. He was a lawyer, and held the office of State's Attorney for Middlesex County from 1797 to 1805. He was elected to Congress for several terms ; had held command of a regiment of State Militia, and was also a Justice of the Peace in town for a number of years. His grandaughter is the wife of Hon. Hiram Willey. His grandson, Wm. O. Mosley, resides in Hadlyme. His father, Thomas Mosley, was quite a popular physician; was a member of the State Medical Association, and was also a Justice of the Peace. Timothy Green, to whom allusion has been made in a former chapter, a resident of the Landing, was afterwards elected to Congress under the District System. These members all proved themselves a credit to the Town, County and State. Captain Green, the father of Timothy, was identified with the early history of the town, as a large landed proprietor was Captain of a company in the Rebellion, the first postmaster in East Haddam, and held many other positions of trust.

The Emmons family which settled on the East Haddam and Colchester turnpike, where Ralph Stark now resides, furnished several prominent men. Among them were Rev. Nathaniel Emmons, who settled in Boston, and acquired a national reputation for power and eloquence as a Congregational minister; and Ichabod, his brother, who moved to Berkshire County, and became somewhat noted as a politician. He was sent to the Legislature for many years, and many anecdotes are related of his wit and humor. He declared at one time, that he should continue going to the Legislature until he had "secured a tax on ministers and jackasses," which were then about the only exemptions, and he kept his word.

Edward Dorr Griffin, who was born near Nathan Jewett's, became a brilliant light in the ministry, a Doctor of Divinity, and President of Williamston College in Massachusetts. His brother, George Griffin, became equally brilliant as a lawyer, and was for many years a member of the bar in New York City, where he amassed a fortune of several hundred thousand dollars by legitimate practice alone. As a birth-place and residence of the legal fraternity, East Haddam has been quite famous. In addition to those where reference has already been made, I will mention such names as I can recall to mind.

Gen. Dyer Throop was the first judge of the County Court for Middlesex County. He held the office from 1785 to 1789. Previous to this, he held the office of Justice of the Peace. At the close of the Revolutionary War, he commanded the 24th Regiment of Connecticut Militia. He died June 4, 1789, at the age of 51.

Francis M. Cone, who died in Georgia a few years since, (the oldest son of Joshua Cone,) was, perhaps, one of the most brilliant men ever raised in this town. He was a distinguished lawyer, afterwards elected to the office of Judge of the Supreme Court, in the State of Georgia, which position he filled with great credit.

William Hungerford, was born in Hadlyme. He graduated at Yale College in 1809, and chose the profession of the law. After practicing for some years in his native town, he removed to Hartford, where he resided at his death. He wore the honorable title of LL. D., and stood for many years at the head of the Hartford bar.

Wm. D. Shipman was a native of Chester; taught school in New Jersey, where he married ; studied two years for the ministry. He afterwards moved to East Haddam, where he studied and practiced law for four years, residing in the house now occupied as the northern part of Maplewood Music Seminary. In 1850 he removed to Hartford, and in 1853 was appointed U. S. District Attorney. He has for some years held the position of Judge of the U. S. Court for the District of Connecticut.

Hon. Eliphlet A. Bulkley, resided at the same house, which took the name of the "Bulkley House." He practiced law for several years in East Haddam, where he had good success. He afterwards moved to Hartford, where he continued his practice and became very wealthy. He graduated in Yale College, in 1824, and is placed upon the records of the Lionian Society as the "Hon. Eliphalet Adams Bulkley, Pres. Soc. Fellow Y. C. Sen. Conn., from East Haddam."

Moses Culver, of East Haddam, read law with E. A. Bulkley ; was admitted to the bar in this County, in 1845; commenced practice in Colchester same year, and continued there till 1846, when he opened an office in East Haddam. While here he held the office of Judge of Probate, and U. S. Commissioner for several years; represented the town in the General Assembly in 1854. In May, 1856, he moved to Middletown, and in 1856 or '58 was appointed State's Attorney, which position he held very creditably for six years. In 1860, he represented the Town of Middletown in the General Assembly. And in 1874 was appointed Judge of the Superior Court. Judge Culver died recently in Middletown.

John C. Palmer, another prominent lawyer of Hartford, and President of the Sharp's Manufac uring Co., was raised in East Haddam, where he practiced law for many years.

CHAPTER XXIV.

The following statistics of the wealth and agricultural products of the town, also the list of offi cers which form the political machinery necessary to run a Connecticut town, may interest some of the old people who have long resided in other States ·

Population of the town in 1870, 2,952.

Divided by estimation as follows :

First Society, 2,140, Second Society, 571, Third Society, 241

No. of Families..534
   "   "   Dwellings..484
   "   "   Colored persons.............. 38
   "   "   Persons over 80.......................... 35
Death by Consumption............................. 20
   "   "   Typhoid Fever............................. 6
   "   "   other causes................................ 28
Rate of mortality to population .. . .1 in 73
No. of stores..................................17
   "   "   Hotels..... 3
   "   "   Churches....................................6
   "   "   Cotton factories...........................14

1 Sash and Blind factory, 1 manufactory of wagon materials, 1 spoon manufactory, 1 silver-plating factory, 1 coffin trimmings factory, 1 cigar manufactory, 1 axe helve and 1 box manufac- tory—

Machine Shops.......... 3
Blacksmith Shops.......... 5
Sawmills...............................7
Gristmills. 4

Value of Real Estate $1,342,250
"   " Personal Estate.......................1,523,324
                                                        ⸺
            Total............................$2,865,574
No. of Horses..................................313
"   " Milch Cows........................ 842
"   " Working Oxen.......................... 638
"   " other cattle................................1138
"   " Sheep.... 1564
"   " Swine..477
Value of Live Stock........................ ......$166,143
Bushels of Wheat raised.............................115
"   " Rye   " 1181
"   " Oats   " 5586
"   " Buckwheat raised.........................1115
"   " Potatoes   " 19429
"   " Corn   " 10439
Pounds of Tobacco   " 66849
"   " Butter 60651
"   " Cheese 4885
"   " Hops 91
"   " Honey 707
Tons of Hay raised........... ....,...............5425
Gallons of Sorgham raised............................226
"   " Wine 294
"   " Milk sold...................... 7440
Value of farm productions.......................$191,701
Value of animals slaughtered.................. 36,895

The grand levy of East Haddam for 1884 is as follows :

616 houses................................. ..... $326,640
30,435½ acres................................. ... 268,369
68⅔ mills 197,130
360 horses.......................... 17,955
1,763 neat cattle.................................. 37,369

Sheep... 1,733
223 carriages.................................. 9.290
Watches and jewelry. 3,880
Musical instruments........................... 4,705
Furniture and books 1,460
Bank and other stocks.......... 238,489
Railroad and other bonds... 23,950
Amount in trade............................... 27,950
Investments in manufacturies.................. 46,550
　　　"　　" Commerce...................... 8,800
Money at interest............... 85,834
　" 　on hand,............................... 11,072
Not specified................................. 25,124
10 and 20 per cent. added..................... 23,825
                                               ─────────
                                               $1,365,110
Deducted by Board of Relief 7,283
                                               ─────────
Total grand levy................. .... $1,357,827

There is an increase of the total of $1,492 over
last year. There seems to be 2½ less houses than
last year; 77½ acres of land less, 1⅓ mills, 33
horses, 303 neat cattle and 19 carriages. Of values:
land, $4,462 less than last year; horses, $1,082 less;
neat cattle, $5,782 less; carriages $190 less.

───────

The officials of the town, elected annually, are as
follows ·

Three Selectmen.
One Town Clerk.
One Treasurer.
Three Assessors.
Three Board of Relief.
One Collector.

One Town Agent.
One Register of Births, Marriages and Deaths.
Two Registers of Voters.
One Agent Town Deposit Fund.
One Treasurer Town Deposit Fund.
Five Constables.
Six Grand Jurors.
One Sealer of Weights and Measures.
Six Hay wards. (Called in the vernacular "Hog Howards.")
Four Key Keepers.
Two Inspectors of Wood and Lumber.
Twelve Sextons.
Two Gaugers.
Four Members Board of Education.
One Auditor.
One School Fund Treasurer.
Six Justices of the Peace.
One Judge of Probate.

In addition there are two Commissioners of Ferries, who hold office by appointment, and a Deputy Sheriff, who is a County officer. A Keeper of the Town's Poor is appointed by the Selectmen. The Board of Health, Fence Viewers, and some other minor positions are held by virtue of the elective offices. Then, each of the seventeen school districts has its set of officials—Committeman, Collector and Clerk. So there are about offices enough to go around.

The present Judge of Probate of East Haddam, Julius Attwood, is the longest in the office of any Judge in the State, having held it for thirty consecutive years.

CHAPTER XXV.

INDUSTRIES.

Though the plough, the axe and the ox-wagon may be regarded as the leading emblems of East Haddam industry—the two latter being an adjunct of the ship-building trade—the spindle, the loom and the crucible have borne an important part. The former implements, many years ago, began to rust, by reason of the exodus of so many young men from the rugged hill sides to the busy centres of civilization. The population however has been kept about evenly balanced by the immigration of skilled artisans to fill the busy mills, which fine water privileges made possible and profitable.

The cotton manufacturing interests have centered about Moodus, which, with Leesville, has maintained twelve cotton factories for several years. The metal industry has been located at Goodspeed's Landing. The various enterprises will only be briefly summarized.

The oldest cotton mill in Moodus was the "Granite Twine Mill," erected in 1815.

The mill now owned by Harper Boies, and known as the Yankee Twine Mill, was established by Capt. Asa Smith, in 1819. He was succeeded by Watrous B. Smith. After many vicissitudes, caused by reverses of fortune, and destruction by fire, the property passed into the possession of Harper Boies, the present owner, who, by good management, has made it a valuable plant.

BROWNELL'S MILL was started by Brownell & Co., in 1825, when they erected a wool carding and cloth dressing building on the site of the present mill. Edward P. Brownell died in 1875, and the business has since been conducted by Charles E., his son.

Stanton S. Card was one of the pioneers in the manufacturing interests of Moodus. He built the mill just south of the "Yankee Twine," and the Southern Mill towards the Cove.

In 1840, Jonathan O. Cone, and Emory Johnson, sons-in-law of Mr. Card, organized as Card & Co. Mr. Card died in 1867. Mr. Cone sold the upper mill to Albert E. Purple, who has ably managed it ever since. Mr. Johnson took the lower mill. He also, about 1860, built the "Neptune Twine Mill," a large structure between the two former, and has since run them both quite successfully. The Neptune Mills employ some thirty hands, with a monthly pay roll of about $1,000. A shop for the manufacture of coffin trimmings, also several dwellings, have been erected by Mr. Johnson. The place has been localized by having a post office and a name—Johnsonville.

The Union Manufacturing Co. was organized in 1829. The New York Net and Twine Co. is an outgrowth of the Smith Manufacturing Co. In 1869 it was reorganized as the "Nichols Co." Ebenezer Nichols, born 1770, was one of the founders of seine twine manufacturing. His son, William E., was born in 1806. He studied medicine, but abandoned the profession for manufacturing. He invented and obtained a patent for "Patent or hand-laid Twine," out of which he got rich. In 1869, he associated with him Demorest and Joralmon, of New York City, and Z. E. Chaffee, of Moodus, and the "Nichols Co." became the "New York Net and Twine Co." Dr. Nichols built a fine residence just south of the Center Congregational Church. He was for many years one of the largest tax-payers in town. Deacon William E. Cone was for many years his efficient business manager.

THE MOODUS MANUFACTURING CO. was organized in 1848 by Harvey & S. B. Chace, of Valley Falls, Mass. They manufactured print cloths, and their works, which are probably the most extensive in the town, stand at the junction of Moodus River and Wigwam Brook. The business was, for many years, superintended by Wm. H. Crowningshield.

The Atlantic Duck Mill was incorporated in 1851, with a capital stock of $10,000, which was afterwards increased to $50,000.   It stands near the Falls, and is the second mill on the stream.

THE WILLIAMS DUCK Co. was organized in 1855, with a capital stock of $30,000, which was afterwards increased to $38,000, all paid in.   It is a fine property, nominally managed by Jehial Wil liams, but practically by Mr. John Barber, under whose able supervision, it is "run for all it is worth."

THE EAST HADDAM DUCK Co. is fully de-scribed in Chapter XI.

The works have been for many years superin-tended by Mr. Nelson Bowers, a gentleman of good business ability, and prominent in town affairs.

THE PINE BROOK DUCK Co., across the Haddam line, was organized by Daniel Wetherell, in 1861. It was destroyed by fire in 1871.

BOARDMAN & SON, Spoons, Plated Ware, etc. Luther Boardman, born in Rocky Hill, commenced manufacturing britannia spoons in a small building in Chester ; moved to East Haddam in 1842. Their extensive works are located at Goodspeed's Land-ing.   When in full operation they employ fifty operatives, with a monthly pay roll of $3,000. Mr. Boardman has been prominent in town and State affairs.   His son, Norman L., was admitted to the firm soon after he became of age, and has always been active in the management of the business. He married the oldest daughter of Daniel B. Warner and built a fine residence near his father. Both father and son and their wives are always liberal in works of practical benevolence, and are widely known throughout the State.

JAMES S. RAY, a native of Haddam, worked at Boardman's for a number of years, and about 1852 started for himself in a small shop at Goodspeed's Landing. Being shrewd, and having an inventive genius, he prospered and "builded greater" until he established a fine business in spoons, forks, coffin trimmings, etc. Some years ago he bought a farm on the hill overlooking the village, put up a fine residence and devoted himself to farming. He also built a yacht, and spends considerable time in summer on the water. Boardman and Ray are neighbors and good friends. The former always has a good team and enjoys riding. He seldom or never steps in a boat. He had rather swim. Ray will have nothing to do with a horse. When he cannot go in his boats he will walk.

"Many men of many minds," says the old copy-book.

WILBUR J. SQUIRE, after many years labor, invented and perfected a machine for knitting gill-nets. He commenced manufacturing in a small shop at Goodspeed's about 1872. He afterwards erected a nice building, and, having a monopoly, did a fine business. He sold out, in 1885, to a Boston company.

———

CHARLES A. CHESTER, after running a shingle mill for many years, at Hadlyme, put up a mill for turning all kinds of handles, about 1870.

———

LODGES, ETC.

COLUMBIA LODGE, No. 26 F. & A. M., was established in 1794, and is one of the oldest in the State. The first communication was held at Oliver Attwood's Hall, where Martin Watrous's store now stands. Meetings were also held in the dwelling now occupied by Dr. Harris. The present membership is about sixty-five. Its lodge room is over Pratt's store at East Haddam Land ing.

———

MIDDLESEX LODGE OF I. O. O. F. was instituted April 22d, 1840, in Moodus, at the house now occupied by William Gates. For many years it has been in a flourishing condition, and has done a great deal of charitable work. None of its sick members ever want for nursing or money. It maintains a good library which is well patronized. Its rooms are over Seward's (formerly Smith's) store, at Goodspeed's.

THE BANK OF NEW ENGLAND was organized in 1854. Changed to National Bank of New England, in 1865. Its capital is $130,000—surplus, $40,000. Julius Attwood, Pres., Thomas Gross, Jr., Cashier.

THE MOODUS SAVINGS BANK was incorporated in 1867.—It has prospered from the start.

THE CONNECTICUT VALLEY ADVERTISER was founded in 1869 by E. Emory Johnson. It was first published at the residence of the owner and afterwards moved to the basement of the Machimoodus House, where these chapters were published in their original form. About 1873, it was purchased by Joseph E. Selden, who has since managed it very successfully. It is one of the most popular country papers in the state. The editorial sanctum is in a new building on the Plain, opposite the Baptist church.

MAPLEWOOD MUSIC SEMINARY was established at East Haddam Landing by Prof. Dwight S. Babcock, about 1865. For twelve years it was conducted with marked success, and filled with ladies from all parts of the country. The site and build ings occupied are referred to in Chapter III. Between the two dwellings, a large Opera House was built with all the modern appointments. The course was a full and thorough one, and the operas give by the school at the close of each term attracted friends of the school and pupils from all directions. The severe attack of malaria, which visited the river towns a few years ago and entered nearly every household, was fatal to the school. With a loss of patronage, financial· difficulties followed, and the property passed into other hands, much to the regret of every citizen. The malarial troubles have now (1887) to a great extent abated, and certain business interests which have long been quiet are also looking more healthy The various "shops" at Goodspeeds are feeling the effects of better times, and the hum of the cotton factories in Moodus is more pronounced. When ship-building revives as a nationl industry, there is reason to believe the two Landings will feel its influence.

The peculiar soil necessary to the raising of the finer qualities of seed-leaf tobacco was discovered a few years ago in many East Haddam farms, and materially adds to the income of the owners.

May prosperity and happiness still attend the good old town ! So say we all.

THE END.

Made in the USA
Middletown, DE
12 January 2019